The Gardener's Guide to Growing

MAPLES

The Gardener's Guide to Growing MAPLES

James Harris

David & Charles
Newton Abbot, Devon

TIMBER PRESS
Portland, Oregon

PICTURE CREDITS

Clive Nichols: pp.2 (Westonbirt Arboretum), 122, 140 (Bath Botanical Gardens), 142–3 (Westonbirt Arboretum), 147 (Tatton Park), 150 (Pyrford Court)
plates by Karl Adamson, all other photographs by Justyn Willsmore

NOTE

Throughout the book the time of year is given as a season to make the reference applicable to readers all over the world. In the northern hemisphere the seasons may be translated into months as follows:

Early winter	December	*Early spring*	March	*Early summer*	June	*Early autumn*	September
Midwinter	January	*Mid-spring*	April	*Midsummer*	July	*Mid-autumn*	October
Late winter	February	*Late spring*	May	*Late summer*	August	*Late autumn*	November

First published in the UK in 2000 by David & Charles Publishers,
Brunel House, Newton Abbot, Devon
ISBN 0 7153 1094 1

First published in North America in 2000 by Timber Press Inc.,
133 SW Second Avenue, Suite 450, Portland, Oregon 97204, USA
ISBN 0-88192-484-9

A catalog record of this book is available from the Library of Congress.

Designed and edited by Jo Weeks
Illustrated by Coral Mula
Printed in Italy by Lego SpA

page 1 A. *cissifolium* (p.60).

page 2 Autumn in the acer glade at Westonbirt Arboretum in Gloucestershire.

page 3 A. *buergerianum* (p.55).

CONTENTS

FOREWORD

I was brought up on maples and have had a passion for them all my gardening life. It is, perhaps, not surprising that one of the oldest and largest trees at Hergest Croft is *Acer pseudoplatanus*, the much-despised sycamore. This was planted around 1800, one hundred years before the garden was started, and is still vigorous and fertile.

When my grandfather began to plant the garden in 1896, maples provided the backbone of much of his early planting. Japanese maples were much used and unlike some of the 'dwarf' conifers with which they were intermingled in the original rockery, they have grown old gracefully and remain ornamental in the garden today. *Acer palmatum* 'Sango-kaku' is many visitors' choice as the most beautiful tree here. With its red winter twigs, its flush of young yellow-green leaves and its golden autumn colour, it is a plant for twelve months of the year.

My grandfather planted many of the larger species as well, including a number of great rarities, and my father continued the tradition. He took great pleasure in *Acer giraldii*, probably an original introduction by Ernest 'Chinese' Wilson for Veitch's nursery. Before its recent reintroduction, there were thought to be only three specimens in Britain, but when he visited Dawyck in Scotland, my father noticed one, almost swamped in a sea of rhododendrons. Finding that the owner was away, he hung a luggage label on the tree. On it was written: 'This is not a sycamore'.

I have become captivated by the beauty of the 'snake bark' maples, whose waxy barks and brilliant young growth mark them as a distinct group of species. Their distribution is a botanical evolutionary puzzle, with one species, *Acer pensylvanicum*, growing on the east coast of North America and all the others in China and Japan.

James Harris's book covers the whole range of this diverse genus and provides a cornucopia of information about its members. Maples are suitable for those with gardens, either great or small (or, come to think of it, those with no gardens at all, as many of them make excellent subjects for bonsai). He has been growing maples for more than 25 years and can thus claim an intimate knowledge of their charms and foibles. Not everyone will agree with his taxonomy but this in no way detracts from this book: after all the 'correct' name is known to botanists and not to plants and he has helpfully indicated where differences of opinion exist.

I hope this comprehensive book will encourage more gardeners to experiment with growing different species of this delightful and diverse genus, and that maples will give them as much pleasure as they give me.

Lawrence Banks, Hergest Croft, April 2000

A. *pseudosieboldianum* is a handsome small tree with leaves that turn rich tints of crimson in the autumn.

INTRODUCTION

"Fragrant leaves blown by the blast,
Blazing brocade over the river,
Oh, the real delight of Tatsuta."

Noin Hoshi, Japan AD988–1050

The passion that people have for maples is revealed by this poem, written by a Japanese monk in the eleventh century. For many years, the Japanese have had a deep affection for the maple, which they call 'Momiji'. They are not alone – the hills and mountain slopes of many lands are ablaze with the fiery colours of maples in the autumn. In Britain gardens and parks are graced by maples with their beautiful leaves, which are often finely and delicately cut. Many maples also have a spring display that is almost as attractive as that of the autumn. And there are those that have wonderful bark: in *Acer palmatum* 'Sango-kaku', it is crimson-pink and in *A. griseum* it is cinnamon-coloured; there are also the snake bark maples with their striped barks. The blooms may not be as showy as those of the magnolias, cherries and other spring plants, but many maples do have very beautiful flowers. For example, the yellow flowers of *A. platanoides* appear just as the leaves open and the upright spikes of greeny-yellow flowers produced by *A. velutinum* are like candles on a Christmas tree; there are also the striking purple-white flowers of *A. circinatum*.

Maple wood has been found to be of the highest quality with the most decorative grain. Pliny wrote: "the maple for the elegance and fineness of the wood is next to the very cedar itself. There are several kinds of it especially the white which is wonderfully beautiful. This is the French maple and grows in that part of Italy that is on the other side of the Po beyond the Alps. The other has a curled grain so curiously maculated, that from a mere resemblance, it was usually called 'The Peacock's Tail' (*Naturalis Historia*). Many famous tables were constructed ...."

John Evelyn also praises the maple. He writes "*Acer* minus the Maple was of old held in equal estimation almost with the Citron, especially the Bruscombe, the French Maple and the Peacock Tail Maple which is that sort, so elegantly undulated and crisped into a variety of curls as emulates the famous Citron. It were a most laudable attempt if some would enquire out and try the planting of such sorts as are not indigenous amongst us ... especially the German Aier and that of Virginia not yet cultivated here but an excellent tree" (*Silva* or a *Discourse of Forest Trees*, 1662).

Such is the veneration people hold for maples, that Canada has adopted the sugar maple (*A. saccharum*) as its national emblem, and several provinces in Japan have taken the maple as their provincial tree.

I became interested in maples about 25 years ago, after the purchase of an old orchard into which I was planning to plant some more interesting and attractive trees. I had always admired the maples at Westonbirt Arboretum and it was not long before I became captivated by this wonderful group of trees. At first, I collected the species but then I met J. D. Vertrees of Oregon, a passionate collector of Japanese maples. He introduced me to these fascinating and beautiful plants and I introduced him to the species.

Discovering maples was like opening a treasure chest. What joy they bring!

A. palmatum 'Tamukeyama' has cascading branches clothed with heavily dissected and richly coloured foliage.

1

THE BOTANY OF MAPLES

Maples, known botanically as *Acer*, belong to the family Aceraceae. This family contains two genera: *Dipteronia* and *Acer*.

There is some obscurity about the origin of the word *Acer*. However, it is known that this was used by the Romans. Ovid tells us that the wood was used for making writing tables on account of its hardness and firmness. Horace, using the adjectival form '*acernus*', also writes about tables made of maple wood.

Philip Miller (1691–1771) wrote: "*Acer* is called according to Vossius (Gerhard Johann Vossius 1577–1649) from *acris* because of the very great hardness of the wood." Loudon (1838) also says that the name means extremely hard. However, some authors suggest it means sharp: *acer* is another Latin word meaning sharp or pungent. Or it could be derived from the Greek ακ (*ak*) or ακρος (*akros*). But, this means highest or topmost – for example, 'ακροπολις' (*acropolis*), meaning a high citadel. The Greek word for maple, by contrast, is σφενδαμνος (*sphendamnos*). It is used by Theophrastus, who describes the wood as valuable for making beds and constructing yokes for beasts of burden.

The genus name *Acer* was confirmed by Linnaeus in *Species Plantarum* (1753) and has been in general use since then.

The word maple derives from the Anglo-Saxon *moepul*. Chaucer uses *mapulder*. In medieval Latin, acers are commonly referred to as *clenus*. This is reflected in the Russian language, where maple is KPEH (*kljen*).

Growing to around 30m (100ft), *Acer platanoides* makes a majestic specimen tree.

THE GENUS

There are at least 120 species belonging to the genus, as well as many varieties, subspecies and cultivars. The best-known and most popular group is that of the Japanese maple (*A. palmatum*) with over 250 cultivars and more being introduced each year.

Trees

Maples are for the most part deciduous trees; there are some evergreen trees as well. They are rarely shrubs. They are diverse in their shape and height. The European maples, which include *A. platanoides* and *A. pseudoplatanus*, are majestic trees growing to 30m (100ft) or so, and being round-headed in outline. These are complemented by many other magnificent maples, for example *A. macrophyllum* from the western United States and *A. mono* from Korea and Japan. Both of these grow to over 28m (75ft). *A. giraldii* and *A. lobelii* are further examples of tall maples (they grow to around 15m/50ft), but they have open crowns.

In their native lands, maples often grow to a much larger size than they do in cultivation, due to the climate and soil conditions. *A. serrulatum* comes from Taiwan, where it grows to over 28m (75ft), but it is much smaller in cultivation. The reverse can also be the case, with a cultivated plant sometimes growing larger than one in the wild.

There are also many maples of much lesser stature. They may be described as small or medium-sized trees and are much more suitable for growing in smaller gardens. Again, they have various shapes and outline. *A. palmatum* 'Sango-kaku' and *A. micranthum* are examples of upright, small trees; they both grow to 6m (20ft). *A. monspessulanum*, by contrast, is a neat, round-headed tree of a medium size, making about 10m (30ft) high.

Almost the only upright species is A. *lobelli*, although there is a number of other examples of fastigiate maples, including A. *platanoides* 'Columnare' and A. *rubrum* 'Columnare'. Dwarf varieties or cultivars have also occurred – for example, A. *platanoides* 'Nanum'.

Shrubby maples

The shrubby maples include, A. *ginnala*, A. *tataricum* and A. *circinatum*. However, the largest group of shrubby maples are the varieties and cultivars of A. *palmatum* (Japanese maples), and A. *japonicum* (full moon maple). Again, these come in a wide variety of forms and shapes. Growing to 5m (15ft) and wide-spreading, A. *palmatum* 'Bloodgood' makes a large shrub or small tree, whereas A. *palmatum* 'Kotohime' is a small, upright maple to 90cm (3ft) or so. Some Japanese maples are even smaller. A. *palmatum* Dissectum Group and A. *palmatum* 'Omurayama' have pendent branches; the former is the smaller of the two and makes a mound shape.

IDENTIFICATION

One or two special features distinguish maples from other trees and help to identify them.

Buds

Maple buds are various colours and shapes and either have several overlapping (imbricate) scales or two outer scales that touch but do not overlap (valvate).

Colours vary widely. The buds of A. *opalus* and closely related maples are dark brown, as are those of A. *villosum* (syn. A. *sterculiaceum*) and A. *franchetii*. Those of A. *platanoides* are green or sometimes, in its cultivars, purple. The buds of A. *davidii* and A. *taronense* are the most decorative among the maples, being bright crimson or purple.

A. *monspessulanum* makes a neat, round-headed tree and has comparatively small leaves.

Examples of maples with imbricate buds include *A. platanoides* and *A. pseudoplatanus*. These both have rounded obtuse buds with imbricate scales; the side buds of the former lie close and tight to the branches, whereas those of the latter jut out. *A. opalus*, *A. franchetii* and *A. villosum* have large buds with usually seven imbricate scales. By contrast, the imbricate buds of *A. ginnala* and *A. buergerianum* are very small and almost hidden.

Examples of maples with valvate scales include *A. ukuruendense*, which has a large, pointed bud, and *A. cissifolium*, which has a small bud. In each case, the outer pair of scales completely covers the inner.

A. palmatum and *A. japonicum* have two buds together at the tip of the branch – most maples only have one. Infact, the two buds are lateral buds, the terminal buds do not develop.

The buds also help to identify a species. Those of *A. triflorum* and *A. mandschuricum* are long and sharp-pointed, making them easy to distinguish in winter.

Branchlets

In one species, *A. campestre*, the branchlets are often winged or corky. In the majority of species, however, they are smooth; some are glabrous and some are densely pubescent. Branchlets can be brownish, purplish, reddish or simply grey. The young branches of some forms of *A. negundo* subsp. *californicum* have a bluey, waxy bloom. This phenomenon is exhibited by other species, including *A. giraldii*.

Bark

One of maples' greatest riches is the remarkable bark possessed by many species. Particularly beautiful are the snake bark maples, which include *A. davidii* and *A. pensylvanicum*. In the first two, the bark is dark purple with white striations and in the last, green with white striations. The bark of some cultivars of *A. palmatum* is marbled purple and white. That of *A. palmatum* 'Orido-nishiki' is dark purple with pink markings, while that of *A. palmatum* 'Saoshika' is silvery, which is especially beautiful in winter.

Usually the bark is smooth and lightly furrowed. However, there are exceptions. The light brown bark of *A. triflorum* is rough and shaggy, as is the greyish-brown bark of *A. truncatum*. The most notable and striking bark is that of *A. griseum*. It is cinnamon-coloured, peeling off in flakes to reveal a more orange colour underneath. As it ages, it becomes a more orange-brown, but it is always peeling. *A. pseudoplatanus* has a plated bark that does not peel off, but is, nevertheless, very attractive.

The white-striped bark of *A. davidii* is very attractive feature of this small to medium-sized tree.

Like the skin of a chameleon, the bark of maples can also change colour. In summer the bark of *A. grosseri* is green with white striations but in winter it is red with white striations. A variety of *A. mono* has green branchlets which later in the summer turn a rich purple.

Leaf shape

Maple leaves are placed opposite each other on the branch and are simple or compound. Usually they are palmately lobed, usually with five lobes, but often with up to 7–9 lobes although there can be as many as 11; the lobes may be shallowly or deeply cut. Some species

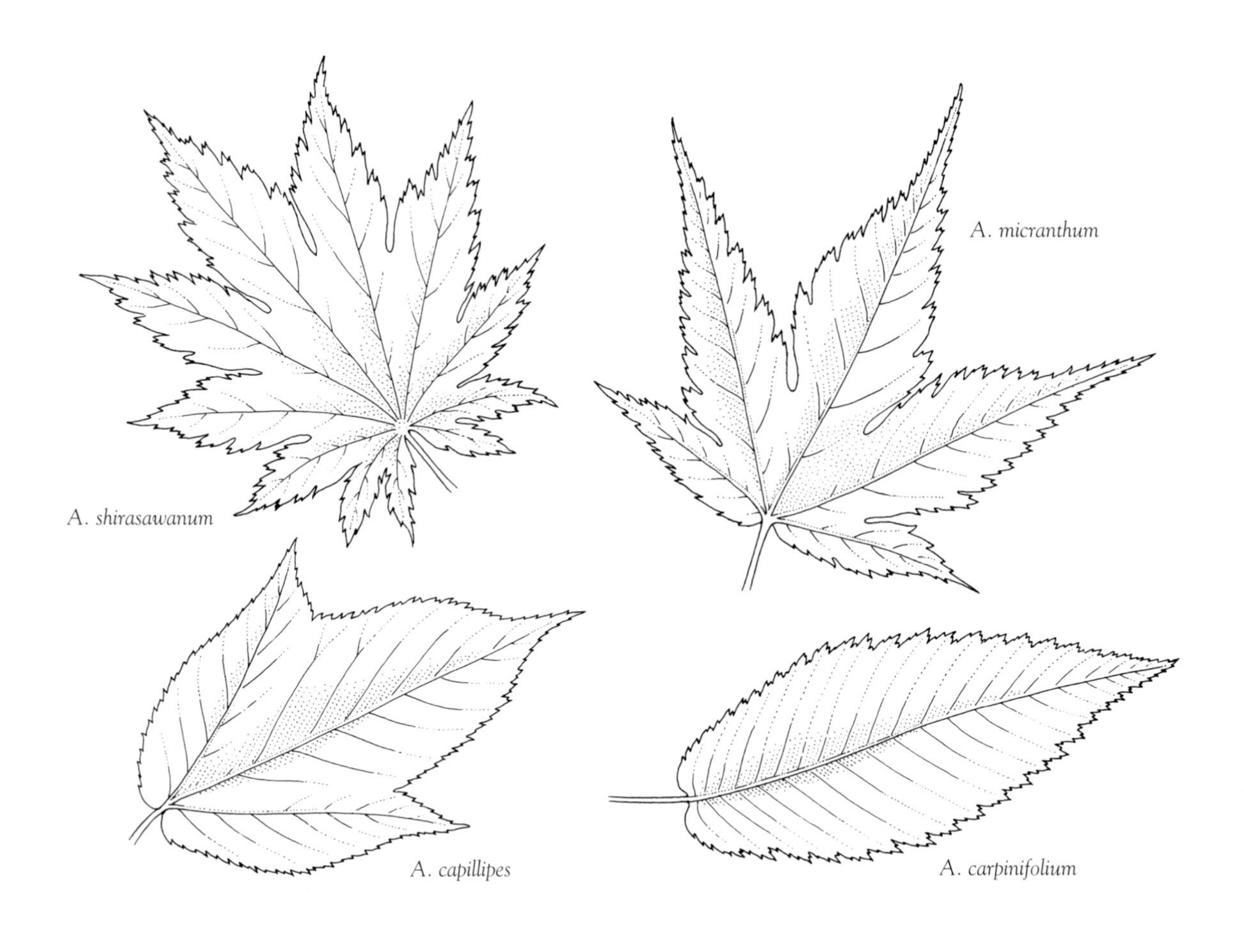

A selection of maples leaves, including entire and palmate types, showing shape and form.

have leaves that are not lobed. For example, those of A. *carpinifolium* are most unusual, being egg-shaped and unlobed. A. *oblongum* and A. *fabri* have similar leaves, but thicker.

A. *circinatum* and A. *sieboldianum* have roundish leaves with broad lobes that are not deeply cut. A. *pentaphyllum* has a remarkable and beautiful leaf, the lobes being very narrow and deeply cut, spreading outwards like an outstretched hand. A. *platanoides* 'Palmatifidum' and A. *saccharinum* 'Laciniatum Wieri' are two other maples with deeply cut lobes. The leaf lobes of the Dissectum Group of A. *palmatum* are often pinnatifid, being deeply cleft to the middle vein.

There is a group of maples with compound leaves, the leaf being divided into three leaflets, and members include A. *triflorum* and A. *griseum*.

The leaves vary from very large to quite small. A. *macrophyllum*, which means 'a large leaf', has a broad palmate leaf, measuring 20–30cm (8–12in) wide. A. *villosum* also has large leaves, 15–22cm (6–9in) across. By contrast, the leaves of A. *monspessulanum*, A. *buergerianum* and some cultivars of A. *palmatum* are quite small, the leaves of the former two species being about 2.5–3.5cm (1–1½in) long and those of A. *palmatum* being as little as 1cm (½in).

Leaf colour

Although most maples have shiny or dull green leaves, there are exceptions. A. *platanoides* 'Crimson King' and A. *palmatum* 'Bloodgood' are among those that have dark purple leaves. There are also yellow-leaved maples. Yellow leaves occur in A. *negundo* 'Kelly's Gold', and those of A. *cappadocicum* 'Aureum' are reddish when they first open in spring, later turning yellow.

Maples with variegated leaves include A. *crataegifolium* 'Veitchii', which has beautiful marbled leaves that are mostly green but have blotches of white or pink. One of the prettiest variegated maples is A. *palmatum* 'Orido-nishiki'. Its leaves are basically cream and pink with white markings, but sometimes the whole leaf is pink. A. *palmatum* 'Higasayama' is remarkable with a spectacular spring display, the pale cream leaflets contrasting with the long and brilliant crimson bud scales.

Wonderful spring colour is a feature of many maples. The opening leaves of A. *palmatum* 'Deshôjô', A. *palmatum* 'Seigen' and A. *palmatum* 'Corallinum' are a brilliant pink, a phenomenon exhibited by many plants from China. A. *truncatum* has attractive reddish-purple leaves in spring, later turning green.

In autumn, maple leaves are a riot of colour, golds and crimson and scarlet (see also p.145).

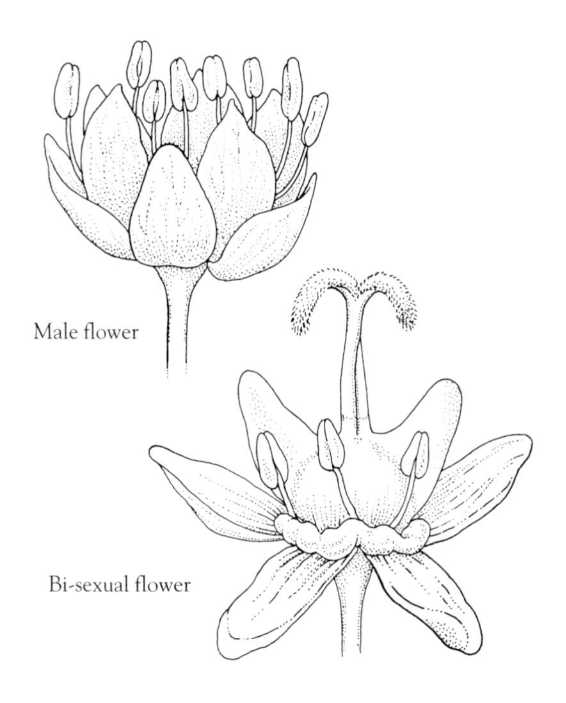

The male flower of A. *ginnala* (top) has stamens only. The bi-sexual flower (above) has stamens and a pistil.

Flowers

As a general rule, maples are not classed as flowering trees. However, some do have attractive spring displays. The yellow flowers of A. *platanoides* and A. *opalus*, coming out just before the leaves, are most striking, while those of A. *circinatum* have beautiful purple stamens. A. *rubrum*, A. *saccharinum* and A. *pycnanthum* flower early in March but most other maples flower in April and May.

Most *Acer* species have flowers with five sepals, together known as the perianth. In many species, the petals and the sepals do not show a great deal of difference of colour and appear greeny-yellow, as in the sycamore. Maples in the Palmatum Group have petals that are greenish-red or red. The bright red petals of the male form of A. *diabolicum* are spectacular. A. *japonicum* 'Aconitifolium' is also very decorative in spring; its large flowers have purplish sepals and are carried on long stalks.

The majority of maples are pollinated by insects. In these species the base of the flower has an organ – the nectiferous disc – which secretes nectar to attract the insects. There are one or two species, including A. *negundo*, that are wind-pollinated. This disc, as well as the sepals, is absent from the flowers of these species.

In general, each flower has eight stamens, but in some species, the number varies from four to ten. In those flowers that are hermaphrodite, the number of stamens is often reduced. Those species with only four stamens include A. *negundo*, A. *cissifolium*, A. *carpinifolium*, A. *argutum* and A. *tetramerum*. The disposition of the stamens is important for the morphological classification of species. According to whether the stamens have their origin on the interior or exterior of the nectiferous disc determines whether the species is intrastamineal or extrastamineal. If the stamens are arranged in an irregular pattern, then their disposition is called amphistamineal.

Usually, the style of the ovary has two stigmas. The partial or total reduction of the style can show the unique male nature of a flower. If one looks at the distribution of the sexes of the flowers in the centre of the same inflorescence, then at first sight it looks as if they are muddled up: male flowers and hermaphrodite flowers exist in the same inflorescence; sometimes, there are also some female flowers. This distribution, which is characteristic of many maples, is called polygamy. In this case, the apparently separate male flowers and female flowers were originally hermaphrodite and one of the organs has already withered away.

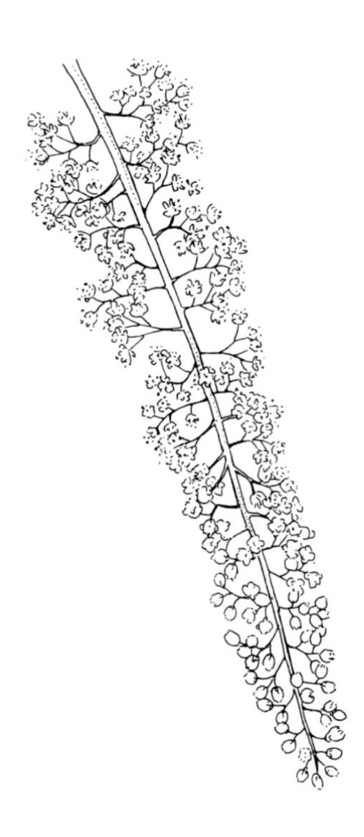

The inflorescence of A. *nipponicum*, which has a racemose formation.

Male flowers and hermaphrodite flowers sometimes appear at different times. For example, the male flowers can occur first at the beginning of the flowering period and the hermaphrodite flowers appear later. Then, towards the end of the flowering, more male flowers can open. This habit of obtaining cross-fertilization by the sexes not being developed simultaneously is known as dichogamy. Other variants can also occur.

The polygamous nature of maple flowers explains why the fruits of A. *griseum* are so often parthenocarpic, that is, without an embryo. This maple has separate male and female flowers in the same inflorescence and so, if circumstances are not right, the female flowers do not pollinate correctly. Despite the fact that there may be no pollination, the fruits begin to form, but they will have no embryo.

Seeds

Many of us have marvelled at maple seeds, which, when they break off in autumn, spin round and round like a helicopter as they fall to the ground (in fact they are often called helicopter seeds). This is one of the most distinctive features of the maple. The fruits are known as keys or samaras and consist of two small nutlets, each with a wing, the wings being joined together at the base. Rarely three fruits are produced together, for example in A. *macrophyllum* 'Kimballiae'.

The fruits of A. *rubrum*, A. *saccharinum* and A. *pycnanthum* ripen in June, while other maples ripen in the autumn.

The size and appearance of the fruits and the angle at which the wings are spread are all good identification features. The nutlets may be quite small, as in A. *crataegifolium*, which has nutlets 4mm (⅛in) in diameter, or large, up to 1.5cm (½in), as in A. *platanoides*. As a rule it can be taken that the larger the leaves are, the larger the fruits will be.

The nutlets are usually round, but they may be flattened. Those of some snake bark maples are concave. They have either smooth, hairy or veined surfaces. Those of A. *tetramerum* are deeply ribbed. Some nutlets have a thin shell but some, for example, A. *griseum* and A. *nikoense*, are hard and woody. Those nutlets with thin shells germinate in the first year, while those with a woody shell usually germinate in the second

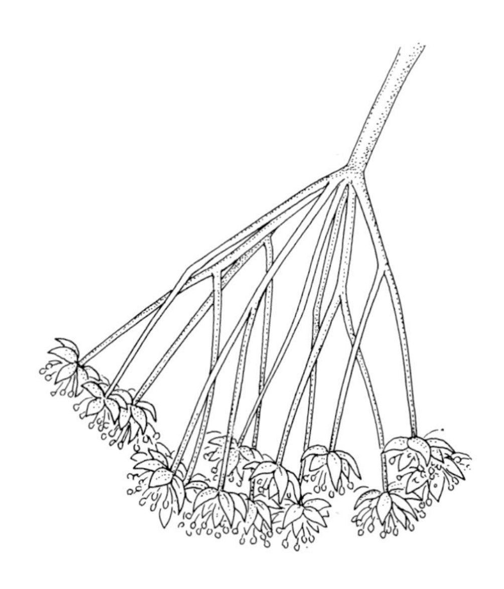

The inflorescence of A. *japonicum*, which has a corymbose formation.

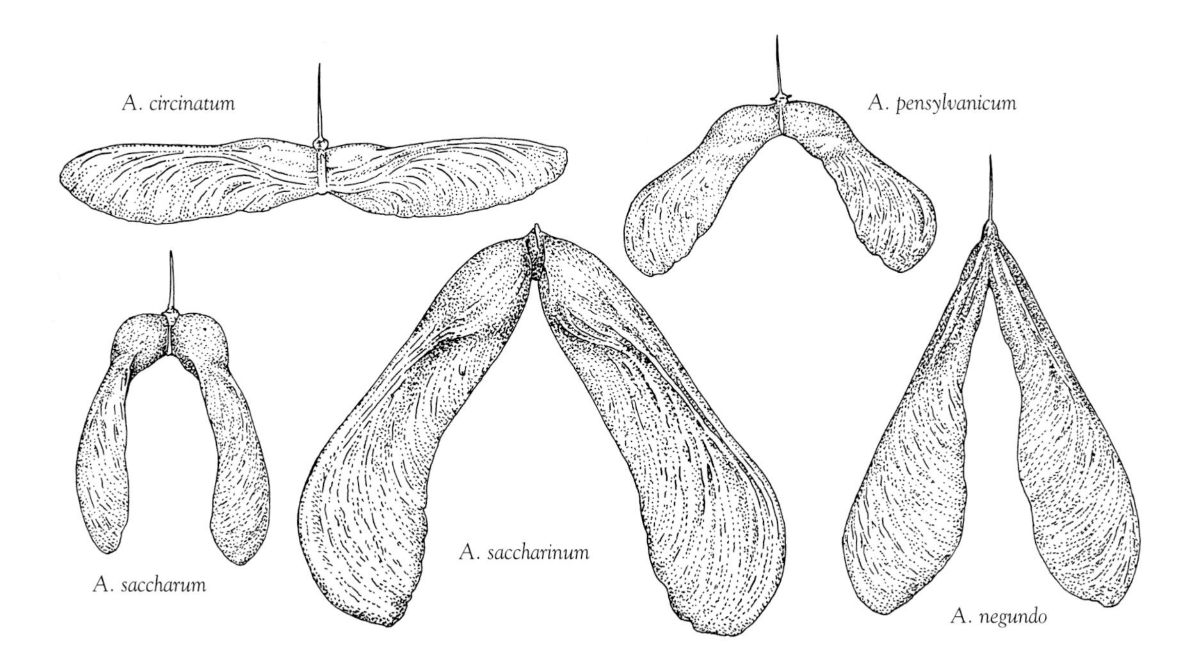

The seeds of maples have wings which help them to be dispersed by the wind. The angle of the wings can be an important aid to identification.

year. Maple seeds are called anemochorous, because they are spread by the wind.

The wings are placed in many different positions. They may be parallel to each other or at any other angle until they are spread horizontally. They are usually reddish, but ripen to brown. Other colours do occur. In autumn, those species that have red wings are most attractive. These include *A. ginnala*, *A. cappadocicum* subsp. *sinicum* and *A. crataegifolium*. Japanese maples have wings that are equally attractive and add to the beauty of many cultivars. The bright red fruits of *A. palmatum* 'Bloodgood' are particularly notable. The fruits of *A. trautvetteri* are also beautiful as they are red and hold their colour for a long time, also in conditions of drought. The fruits of *A. negundo* have translucent wings.

2

HABITAT & ORIGIN

The genus *Acer*, to which maples belong, originated in Palaeolithic times and is widely distributed. However, it is not worldwide in its occurrence: maples are found mainly in northern temperate regions. This is thought to be because of the shift of the continents. In the cretaceous period, the world was very different from today. Since then continents and oceans have moved and temperatures are generally lower than they were. A number of fossilized maple leaves have been found although there have been few finds of fossil fruits.

Maples do not grow throughout northern temperate zones. They are only found where the rainfall is 1000mm (40in) or more. Suitable conditions occur in the mountainous regions of Europe, North America and parts of Asia. The immense development of species in the areas to the west of the Himalayas and in China and Japan has been encouraged by their humid climate. Abundant rainfall also falls in some regions along the coast of the Black Sea.

It is possible that the centre of the origin of maples lies in the Himalayas to south-west China and North Vietnam. A. *tonkinense* is a primitive maple that grows in North Vietnam, which supports this theory. In this survey of the areas where maples grow, I propose to start in the Himalayas.

THE FAR EAST

It is astonishing that Kathmandu lies at the same latitude as Cairo, and has a temperate climate with an average temperature of about 18°C (64°F) and a rainfall of between 150–200cm (60–80in) or sometimes even more. Some maples from this region are tender and do not grow well in Britain, except in Cornwall or in protected conditions; in North America, they will survive in zone 7 or possibly 6. These include A. *oblongum*, A.*villosum* (syn. A. *sterculiaceum*) and its close relative A. *thomsonii*, which is even more tender. The beautiful A. *pectinatum* and A. *caudatum*, which grow at higher altitudes in the Himalayas, are proving more hardy in the British climate.

Despite the fact that the greatest aggregation of *Acer* species grows in China, very few fossil maples have been found there. China was not affected by an ice age and, as a result, it has a remarkably rich and varied flora, including at least 80 species of maple; the number becomes greater if one also counts subspecies and varieties. The range is very wide, too: they are not limited to one or two sections (see pp.45–51), but are to be found spread over nearly all the sections. In addition, it is not unusual to find at least half a dozen species growing together with other trees and plants in a small area in the forests of Sichuan and Hubei (in central China) and Yunnan (in south-west China).

The average temperatures that occur in China are similar to those of Britain, although China has a continental climate, so it can be warmer in the summer and colder in the winter. The warmer summer weather helps to ripen the young wood, enabling the maples to withstand colder winters. The rainfall is about 1000mm (40in).

In many parts of China (Hubei, for example) the soil is alkaline, which is also true of much of the soil in Britain, so many Chinese species are suitable for growing in Britain. A. *davidii*, A. *maximowiczii*, A. *henryi*,

A. *nikoense* (A. *maximowiczianum*) is a native of China and Japan. It was introduced into cultivation in 1881.

A. tetramerum and *A. griseum* are just some of the extraordinarily rich collection of plants to be found in these alkaline areas. These species grow at altitudes of 1500m (5000ft) or more. At lower altitudes *A. sinense*, *A. paxii* and *A. oblongum* are found. These are not so hardy and will not survive temperatures below –20°C (–5°F), but can be found in gardens in south-west England.

The climate in regions of south-west China, such as Yunnan, is more sub-tropical and supports relatively few maples. Bamboo forests are characteristic of this region.

Manchuria in north-east China is the home of several maples, including *A. ginnala*. Temperatures in this area are lower than those in Britain (at Harbin in the north, they average –19°C/–2°F in January), and the hardiness of such plants as *A. ginnala* is well known. *A. mono*, another native of this region, is also very hardy.

A. tetramerum, a native of China, is found growing at high altitudes in alkaline soil in the province of Hubei.

Immediately to the south of Manchuria is Korea, which also enjoys a continental climate. *A. palmatum*, *A. pseudosieboldianum*, *A. triflorum* and *A. mandschuricum* are just a few of the beautiful maples that are indigenous to this region. During the autumn leaf-fall, when the mountainsides are ablaze with colour, one of the most impressive displays is that of *A. pseudosieboldianum*.

To the east of Korea, between the Asian continent and Japan, is the island of Ullung-do. Curiously, its flora is strongly influenced by Japan: many of the plants growing in and endemic to Ullung-do are subspecies of Japanese species. Ullung-do has two endemic maples, *A. okamotoanum* and *A. takesimense*. *A. okamotoanum* is related to *A. mono*, and *A. takesimense* to *A. pseudosieboldianum*.

Further to the east is Japan, a country that lies across a number of latitudes and, as a result, embraces a number of different climatic zones. Hokkaido, the smaller of the two islands, in the north has a much colder climate and here one finds *A. japonicum*, *A. nikoense* (syn. *A. maximowiczianum*), *A. buergerianum* and *A. carpinifolium*. The mountainous centre of Japan has forests of pine, spruce and fir, together with magnolia, zelkova and other trees. Among these are *A. rufinerve*, *A. cissifolium* and *A. nipponicum*. In the south, the climate is more subtropical. Maples that grow here include *A. morifolium*.

Taiwan is south of Japan and Korea, being south-east of the Asian continent. This island lies across the Tropic of Cancer, at the same latitude as the Sahara and Mexico. The centre of the island is mountainous, and, here, at an altitude of over 1000m (3280ft), *A. kawakamii* (syn. *A. caudatifolium*), *A. morrisonense* (syn. *A. rubescens*) and *A. serrulatum* grow in mixed forests. These species will survive quite happily in warmer climates like that of southern Britain. However, *A. albopurpurascens*, which is indigenous to the lower slopes, is not entirely hardy in Britain.

AMERICA

In the Americas, maples grow from Canada down into Mexico. The maples of the Pacific Coast developed

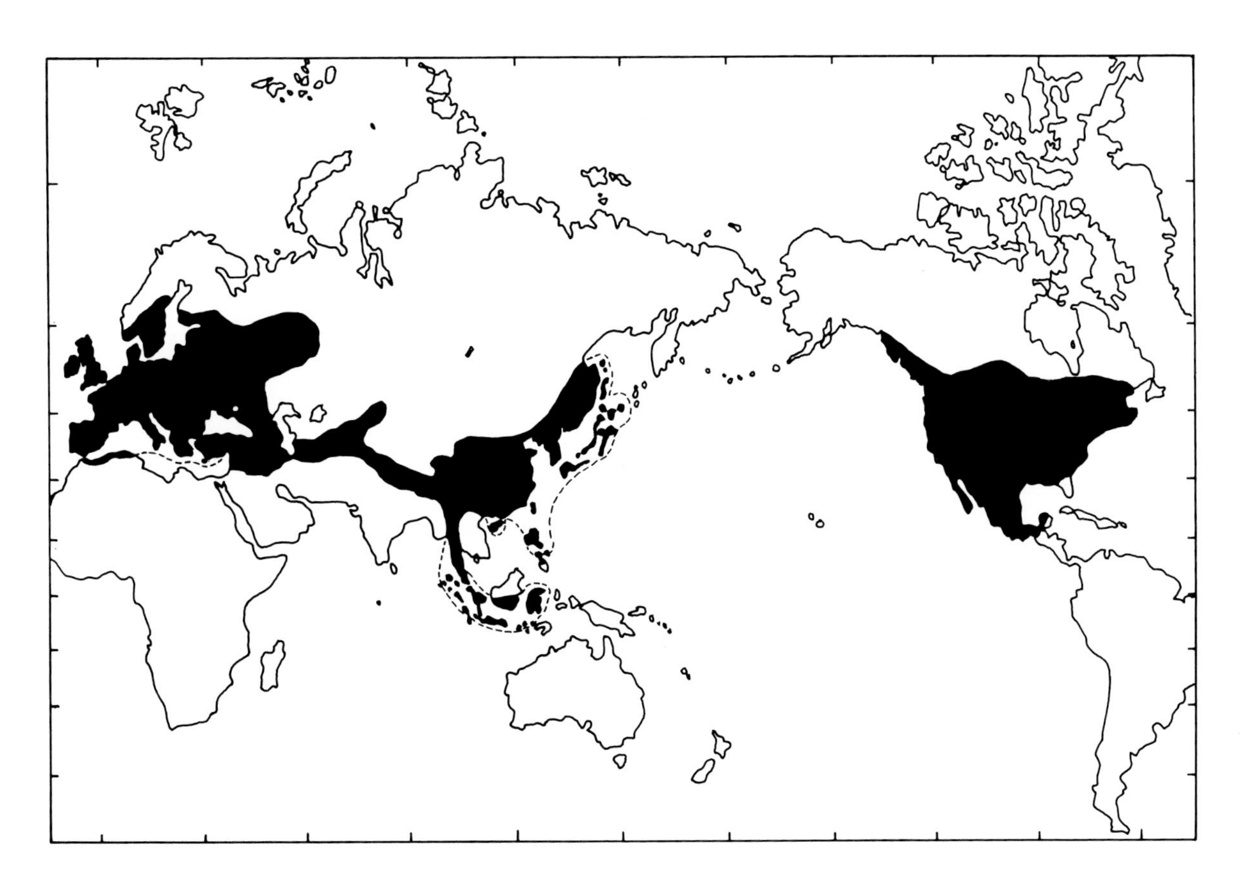

In this map of the world, the geographic distribution of maple species is shaded black.

independently to those in the east. They are not very closely related, and are to be found in different sections (see pp.45–51). *A. macrophyllum* is the only tree-like species that grows in western North America and it occurs in the forests of the north-west in conjunction with the Douglas fir, alder and other trees. The shrubby *A. circinatum* grows not only in the sub-storey at the edges of the forests, but also along riverbanks. Its range extends northwards, almost to Alaska and it is found with willow and alder. *A. glabrum* is indigenous to a similar area and also grows in mountainous regions.

The first maple the early settlers of America would have seen when they landed in the eastern United States was probably *A. negundo*. At first, this was not recognized as a maple – it was called *Negundo fraxinifolia* due to its trifoliate leaves and ash-like fruits. It grows from Vermont down to Mexico, where it is found in the form *A. negundo* subsp. *mexicanum*.

Other tree-like species that are native to the eastern states include *A. rubrum*, *A. saccharinum* and *A. saccharum*. They form part of forests that contain a rich variety of trees and plants and which have changed little over the millennia: the ice age did not encompass the whole of the eastern United States but only the northern parts. *A. saccharum* grows over a greater area of North America than any other maple. It is even found in Mexico as the subspecies *skutchii*. The beautiful, shrubby *A. spicatum*, which occurs in the northern part of the eastern United States, grows in woody forests in assocation with birch, spruce and pine. It is also found along riverbanks.

Plants can provide evidence of the movement of continents. For example, fossil remains of *Ginkgo biloba*, which grows in China and Japan, have been found in the eastern United States. Likewise, there are maples that bear some comparison. For example, *A. rubrum*, which is a native of the eastern United States, is very similar to *A. pycnanthum*, which grows in Japan. Their leaves are almost the same, both flower early in

PLATE I

Acer rubrum *and cultivars and* Acer rufinerve

A. *rubrum* 'Schlesingeri'

A. *rubrum*

All leaves are shown at approximately half lifesize

A. *rubrum* 'Scanlon'

A. *rubrum* 'October Glory'

A. *rufinerve*

A. platanoides, the Norway maple, is a native of Europe and is fairly widespread through the region.

the year and both fruit in June. In addition both these maples have beautiful autumn colour. Likewise, the leaves of the American *A. circinatum* are very similar to those of the Japanese *A. japonicum*. Both species produce two buds together at the end of the branches and have gorgeous autumn colour. *A. pensylvanicum* is the only snake bark maple that is native to North America. It has a similar counterpart in Japan: *A. rufinerve*. However, in these two species, the leaves are quite different – those of *A. pensylvanicum* turn golden-yellow in autumn, while those of *A. rufinerve* are a rich scarlet.

EUROPE

There are several species of *Acer* indigenous to Europe, perhaps the best known are the Norway maple, *A. platanoides*, the sycamore, *A. pseudoplatanus* and the field maple, *A. campestre*.

The Norway maple has a wide distribution, inhabiting the greater part of Europe and also growing to the east as far as the Caucasus. In Norway, where it is known as the 'Lon', it grows in the south where specimens up to 18m (60ft) high have been recorded. It is also found wild in Finland. This species can stand a great degree of cold and is not affected by spring frosts.

The sycamore grows in the Pyrenees, Alps, Carpathian Mountains and other mountains in Germany and Greece. In Russia it spreads along the Black

Sea to the mountains of Crimea. It is usually met as a single tree or in small groups, forming part of the beech and silver fir forests at an altitude of between 300m (1000ft) and 1525m (5000ft). It does not occur naturally on wet ground, or in light soils or heavy clay soils.

A. *campestre* grows generally throughout Europe, but not in the north nor in the Iberian Peninsula, and extends into western Asia, where it is found in the Caucasus.

The Alps formed a barrier at the end of the Ice Age, preventing the spread of plants to the north. After the Ice Age, A. *monspessulanum* and A. *opalus* migrated to south-west Germany and southern Europe, from Portugal to Turkey. These Mediterranean maples prefer warmer climates and grow on drier soils than their northern cousins.

Turkey forms the boundary between Europe and Asia and its forests, which are remains of glacial forests, create an interesting junction between the flora of Europe and the flora of Asia. A number of plants that have been lost to Europe are found in them. Here one finds A. *cappadocicum* and A. *trautvetteri* growing among beech, pine and fir with an understorey of rhododendrons and laurel.

In the Caucasus, A. *divergens*, a close relative of A. *cappadocicum*, is found growing in forests along with A. *velutinum* (syn. A. *insigne*) and A. *trautvetteri*. A. *divergens* and A. *velutinum* occur at altitudes of up to 760m (2000ft), while A. *trautvetteri* grows higher, at between 2300–3000m (6000–8000ft), in company with birch and sub-alpine shrubs.

Across in Afghanistan and Turkestan there are a few indigenous maples, including A. *ginnala* and A. *pentapomicum*.

The maple is absent from the whole of Africa except the north-west along the Mediterranean where one or two maples occur, including A. *campestre* and subspecies of A. *monspessulanum* and A. *opalus*. Only one maple grows south of the equator, this being A. *laurinum*, which is found in the forests of Indonesia.

3

A HISTORY OF THE MAPLE

It is a paradox that the British Isles support only a limited native flora, but have a climate that is ideal for growing the many plants that have been introduced from foreign lands. Britain lies at a more northerly latitude than China or Japan, from where many maples originate, but is warmed by the Gulf Stream, which flows to the west, and as a result, has a temperate climate with a good rainfall that is generally suitable for a wide variety of maples.

The field maple (*A. campestre*) is the only maple that is native to the British Isles. It grew in Britain after the Ice Age and before the land bridge between Dover and Calais was submerged in the waters of the Straits of Dover.

Unlike many other plants, no maples were brought into Britain by the Romans and it was not until the fifteenth century that the first introduction of a maple occurred. Through Mary Queen of Scots, Scotland had a close connection with France and it was in Scotland that the first planting of the sycamore (*A. pseudoplatanus*) was made. Sycamore is native to the mountainous districts of France, the Alps and the Pyrenees. In the past, it was also called the dool or grief tree because powerful barons used its strong branches from which to hang their enemies.

EARLY BOTANICAL EXPLORATION

The Renaissance, which started in the fifteenth century, was a period of revival of interest in the arts and literature, and in the seventeenth century the establishment of a botanic garden in Edinburgh, Scotland was a result of a growth in interest in nature and plants. In 1603 James Sutherland was appointed Intendant of what became the Royal Botanic Garden at Edinburgh, and Loudon attributes the introduction of the Norway maple, *A. platanoides*, to him.

John Tradescant the younger is credited with introducing *A. rubrum* to Britain from North America.

This was also an age of exploration; the first British colony was founded in Jamestown in 1605. One of the earliest travellers in the New World was the elder John Tradescant. The introduction of the red maple, *A. rubrum*, in 1656 is attributed to his son, also John, who was known as the John Tradescant the younger. One of the bishops of London at the time was Dr Henry Compton, who was also head of the church for the American colonies and a great supporter of botanical exploration. Among his missionaries was John Banister, who arrived in Virginia in 1678. He was an all-round naturalist, and it was probably he who was responsible for introducing the ash-leaf maple (*A. negundo*), at first called *Negundo fraxinifolium* because it was not recognized as a maple.

While the British were in the Americas, botanical exploration on the European continent was at first largely concerned with the Levant. In 1623 Joseph Pitton de Tournefort was appointed to the chair of botany in the Royal Garden in Paris and in 1700 he explored Greece, Asia Minor and Armenia.

Trade and botanical discoveries

During the seventeenth century, Europeans were also making every effort to advance trade in various parts of the world. The English East India Company was established and one who entered its service was James Cunningham. He sailed into Chinese waters in 1698. Although he was not able to travel into the interior of the country, he did discover the trident maple (*A. buergerianum*). However, it was not for many years that this plant was introduced into cultivation.

The eighteenth century is noted for being a period when there were many men of great learning. Among these was Philip Miller who was appointed superintendent of the Apothecaries' Garden in Chelsea in 1722. In 1738 Miller introduced the Montpelier maple (*A. monspessulanum*) whose pale yellow flowers are attractive to bees. During his life, Miller introduced two other maples into cultivation, the eastern Mediterranean maple (*A. obtusifolium*) and the tartar maple (*A. tataricum*). The seeds of the latter are made into a food by the Kalmucks, who are nomads of Mongolian origin. They are boiled in water and then mixed with milk and butter.

Also during this century, more maples were discovered in the eastern United States. In 1728 Sir Charles Wager introduced a maple that he called *A. eriocarpum* but which is now more commonly known as the silver maple (*A. saccharinum*). Aiton recorded that the sugar maple (*A. saccharum*) was introduced by Peter Collinson, a draper from London, in 1735. This maple is the national emblem of Canada, its wood has a beautiful grain and is valued for furniture making, and, along with the red maple (*A. rubrum*), it forms one of the chief elements in the glorious colour effects of autumn in that part of the world.

Mark Catesby was the first full-time professional collector of maples whose movements in America are reasonably well recorded. Peter Collinson was one of his closest friends and he asked Catesby to recommend a person to gather seeds in America and send over plants. Catesby recommended John Bartram who was a Quaker, a native of Pennsylvania and a self-taught botanist. Bartram was probably responsible in assisting Archibald, Duke of Argyll to introduce the mountain maple (*A. spicatum*) in 1750, which was first called *A. montanum*. Another beautiful maple from North America, the moose-bark maple (*A. pensylvanicum*), was also discovered at this time. It was introduced into cultivation in 1755 by Messrs Kennedy & Lee of the prominent and famous Vineyard Nursery of Hammersmith, London.

Linnaeus and plant hunting

The famous botanist, Carl von Linné (Linnaeus), who was born in Sweden in 1707, appointed people, whom he called apostles, to go out and find plants for him in foreign lands. Pedro Kalm was sent to America and Carl Peter Thunberg was sent to Japan. Thunberg left Uppsala in Sweden in August 1770 and travelled to Japan by way of South Africa. He joined the Dutch East India Company which was attempting to expand trade in the Far East. Although entry into Japan was still forbidden, foreigners were allowed to land on a tiny artificial island called Deshima in Nagasaki Harbour. There Thunberg was able to collect leaves and plant specimens brought from the mainland to feed the animals, and these specimens formed the basis of his *Flora Japonica* (1784). He provided the first description of *A. palmatum* and *A. japonicum*, which were not brought into cultivation for many more years. After Thunberg left Deshima in 1773, Japan was not returned to by botanists for another fifty years. The next botanist to visit Japan was Siebold, who travelled there in 1826 (see p.31).

NORTH AMERICAN DISCOVERIES

The eighteenth century closed with a remarkable journey of exploration in North America and the nineteenth century opened with another one.

In 1791, the British government, concerned at the increasing Spanish influence on the western United States, sent out an expedition under the command of Captain Vancouver. On board was Archibald Menzies, a surgeon and botanist from Edinburgh. On May 2nd 1792 at Protection Island, Menzies had his first sighting of the big-leaf maple (*A. macrophyllum*). He wrote: "We saw a variety of hardwoods scattered along the banks of the river such as oak, sycamore or great maple, sugar maple, mountain maple and Pennsylvanian maple ...."

The United States of America are split from north to south by the great Mississippi River. This river also acts as a visible dateline for botanical exploration: at the beginning of the nineteenth century it had hardly ever been crossed by botanists. All this changed in May 1804, when the US government sponsored an expedition up the river under the command of Captain Lewis and Captain Clarke, both of whom had some training

The Montpelier maple (*A. monspessulanum*), which was introduced in 1738, is a small tree with a rounded habit.

'Kimballiae' is a cultivar of A. *macrophyllum*, a species discovered in North America in 1826 by David Douglas.

in botany. For several months the expedition worked its way along the river and made a slow ascent towards the Rocky Mountains. It eventually reached the Pacific Ocean on October 7th 1804.

The first plant collection made by the expedition was lost in a river flood but the men made another small collection, which included two species of *Acer* on their way home. This passed into the hands of the Irish-born nurseryman, Macmahon, of Philadelphia and then to the German botanist, Frederick Pursh. In 1814 Pursh published his *Flora Americae Septentrionalis*, in which he described the two maples from the western United States, A. *circinatum* and A. *macrophyllum*.

The next species discovery in North America is credited to Thomas Nuttall, an impecunious journeyman-printer from Liverpool, who arrived in Philadelphia on April 23rd 1808. He is believed to have found A. *grandidentatum* at Mount Timpanagos on the Bear River in Idaho.

In the field of horticulture, Nuttall was far excelled by his contemporary, David Douglas (1799–1834). Douglas, the son of a village stonemason, was born at Scone, Perthshire and trained in private and botanic gardens. In 1823 he was sent to the eastern United States by Joseph Sabine, the Secretary of the Horticultural Society (later the Royal Horticultural Society). He set off for his first season's collection in 1824, sailing on the *Mary Ann* for the Columbia River. The collection was sent to Britain from Oregon in September 1825, also on the *Mary Ann*. (Unfortunately, Douglas was not able to see the ship sail as he had injured his knee on a rusty nail which incapacitated him for some weeks.)

In 1826 Douglas travelled up the Columbia and the Spokane rivers to Kettle Falls. It was during this season that he collected A. *macrophyllum* and A. *circinatum*. In August of that year, on hearing that a ship, probably the last of the season, was to leave for England, he made a rapid journey back from Kettle Falls, travelling 800 miles in 12 days. He arrived in Fort Vancouver looking so weary and ragged that the inhabitants thought some disaster had occurred. A. *macrophyllum* and A. *circinatum* were thus introduced into cultivation and their remarkable history was complete – from their first sighting by Menzies in 1792, collection by Lewis and Clarke in 1804 and, finally, their introduction by Douglas in 1826.

Douglas's adventures continued on another journey in June 1833, when, while on the Fraser River, his canoe was dashed to pieces on some rocks and all his botanical notes, collections and personal possessions were lost. Douglas himself spun in a whirlpool for an hour and forty minutes and it is a miracle that he emerged alive.

In 1827, when he was collecting for Professor J. D. Hooker of the Royal Botanic Gardens, Kew, Douglas found a form of the rock maple in the Blue Mountains: it is named after him A. *glabrum* subsp. *douglasii*. At first Douglas sent only leaf specimens, but later he added more material and so Hooker was able to write in 1847: "I have now received good fructified specimens gathered during poor Douglas's last journey in the Blue Mountains". Douglas had met an untimely end in Hawaii in 1834, when he fell into a pit, into which a bullock had already fallen, and was gored to death by it.

THE FAR EAST

With the possible exception of North America, no country has made so great a contribution to our gardens as China. In the 1830s many important events in the field of botany occurred in the Far East.

While explorers from Europe came in from the south, those from Russia came in from the north. In 1830 the Russian government sent a new ecclesiastical mission to Beijing (Peking). Among those in the mission were three scientific men, one of whom was Dr Alexander von Bunge, an eminent Russian botanist who had also studied medicine. He had been born in Kiev in 1803. In 1831, as well as collecting *A. truncatum* around Beijing, Dr Bunge returned home with many other plant specimens and an interesting collection made in Mongolia. *A. truncatum* was not actually introduced into cultivation until 1881, when the German, Dr Bretschneider sent seed to the Royal Botanic Gardens at Kew. After Dr Bunge's successful visit, no further attempts to obtain Chinese plants were possible until the conclusion of the infamous Opium Wars of 1840–42.

Plant-hunting in Japan was still very restricted. Very different from his predecessor the naïve Thunberg, the arrogant and power-loving German-born Dr Philip Franz von Siebold landed on Deshima on August 11th 1826. Although his interests were mainly in the fields of politics and enthnology, plant hunting, particularly for profit, ran a close third. The Napoleonic Wars had come and gone, Holland had temporarily lost her possessions in the East, and the Dutch were anxious to restore their almost vanished trade. As a skilled physician, von Siebold was an important asset to the Dutch East India Company. Skilled in several sciences, he soon built up a following of pupils and grateful patients and was able to make excursions into inland Japan. It was during these trips that he managed to acquire a good deal of forbidden knowledge about Japanese politics and economics, which eventually led to him falling foul of the Japanese authorities.

Despite the fact that maps of Japan were most strictly prohibited, von Siebold had managed to obtain several during his time in Japan. In 1828 his plant collection was packed for the return journey to Europe. However, the vessel that was to take it and von Siebold from Tokyo to Deshima was beached in a storm and, before it could be refloated, von Siebold's maps were discovered. He was imprisoned for a year and, on his release in December 1829, was permanently banished from Japan. He contrived to send part of his collection back to Holland without him in January 1829. And when he eventually sailed home, he took with him a further collection to Leiden.

Later in life, von Siebold did make a return journey to Japan where he received a herbarium collection of all the cultivars of *A. palmatum* from the Prince of Tsikousen. He took this back with him to Leiden.

It is to von Siebold whom we owe the first description of many of the maples that are to be found growing in Japan. In 1845 he published *Flora Japonicae Familiae Naturales*, describing *A. carpinifolium*, *A. cissifolium*, *A. crataegifolium*, *A. distylum*, *A. micranthum* and *A. rufinerve*. Somehow, some of his material came into the hands of Friedrich Anton Wilhelm Miquel who hurriedly made descriptions of them in order to gain the credit for being the first author. He published *A. sieboldianum* in 1865, followed by *A. buergerianum* in 1867.

A. crataegifolium is among many maples first described by the irrepressible plant-hunter Dr Philip von Siebold.

A. *cappadocicum* is widespread, occurring naturally in the Caucasus, North Turkey and Iran.

India

Another country gaining botanical recognition at this time was India. However, the history of botanical interest in the country was much older, with arguably the first naturalist to study its plants being Alexander the Great (356–323BC) on his Asiatic campaign. (It is known that he wanted his former tutor, Aristotle, to write a book on natural history, and that he employed a special corps in hunting, fishing, hawking and plant collecting.)

The botanic garden at Calcutta was founded in 1786 and its second director was William Roxburgh, who arrived there in 1801. In 1813 Nathaniel Wallich, a Danish surgeon of Jewish extraction, was appointed to assist him. Wallich succeeded to the directorship in 1872. The story of his enormous contribution to botany cannot be told here; what concerns us are his travels and the use he made of native collectors to bring in plants from regions that were inaccessible to Europeans. Many of the Himalayan maples were found and either described or introduced by him. Dr John Forbes Royle (1799–1858) was a surgeon of the East India Company in Bengal, later Curator of the botanic garden at Saharanpur and then Secretary of the Horticultural Society of London. He collected A. *villosum* at Choo Mountain and his native collector Kamroop collected A. *acuminatum* and A. *caudatum*. A. *oblongum* was collected by Wallich himself. Dr George Govern, superintendant at the garden at Saharanpur in the same period, found A. *pectinatum* at Sirmore.

In 1828 Wallich came to Europe, arriving in London with a collection of dried plants, which were distributed among the principal public and private museums in Europe and North America. Some of the material came into the hands of David Don, librarian of the Linnaean Society, who subsequently wrote the pioneer work on the flora of Nepal – *Prodromus Florae*

Nepalensis (1825), in which he published *A. acuminatum*. Other material came into the hands of the young Swiss law student, Alphonse Louis Pierre Pyramus de Candolle. He described *A. oblongum*, which was introduced into cultivation in 1824.

Wallich returned to India in 1832. Three years later he made a trip to Assam, accompanied by Dr William Griffiths and John Mclelland. During this journey, Griffiths discovered *A. thomsonii*, which Miquel (see p.31) published in 1867.

Other important maple discoveries were also being made during this period. *A. cappadocicum* had been collected by Tournefort in Armenia, by Karl Heinrich Emil Koch in the Caucasus and by Carl Anton von Meyer of the University of Dorpeth in Lavonia, in the Talysch Mountains. The latter gave it the name of *A. laetum*, which he published in 1831. In 1837 Friedrich Ernst Ludwig von Fischer, together with Meyer, published *A. hyrcanum*, which he had collected, also in the Talysch Mountains. This maple was introduced into cultivation in 1869.

A GOLDEN AGE

The last forty years of the nineteenth century were perhaps the most exciting in the history of plant hunting. New frontiers were opened and explorers and plant collectors poured into those countries where entry had previously been forbidden.

Japan and Korea

In 1853 Commodore Matthew Perry of the United States sailed into Tokyo harbour in his flagship *Vincennes* and put on such an imposing show of force that the Japanese government realized that a policy of isolation could no longer be maintained. Immediately, two ports were opened and an American consul established. At the same time, Korea also opened its frontiers. Botanists and explorers came flocking in. Among the first to arrive was John Gould Veitch from Britain, who sailed into Nagasaki in July 1861.

China

The French sent out a number of missionaries to China, one of whom was Armand David, a Jesuit, who was attached to the mission of the Lazarists in Beijing in 1862. David, an all-round naturalist with a preference for zoology, is credited with introducing many new animals, including the panda. With a stoic disregard of local insurrections and his own constitution, he made three journeys in China. Travelling was difficult and transport hard to obtain – one night his donkey had to be taken into the tent to keep it safe from wolves.

His travels paid dividends, however. In April 1868 he found a maple in Moupine in the province of Sichuan. Franchet named it *A. davidii*, after him. The same species was later introduced by Maries, who collected seed near Ichang in the province of West Hubei in 1879. David recorded in his diaries that he found a maple in the province of Kiangsi and that Maximowicz (see below) named it *A. ulmifolia*, but the plant appears to be the same as *A. davidii*. In Mongolia David collected *A. tataricum* and *A. lobelii*. The latter would appear correctly to be *A. cappadocicum* var. *sinicum*, which was also collected by Henry in the 1880s (see p.38). (*A. lobelii* had already been described as an Italian native in 1583.)

As well as Armand David, other French missionaries sent to China in the mid-nineteenth century include Father Jean Marie Delavay, who was appointed to Hui Chou in the southern province of Kwantung in 1867. He was a keen botanist and collected thousands of plants on Mount Tsemei, which he called his garden. Among the many he sent back to France was *A. paxii*.

Paul Guillaume Farges went to the *Mission Etranger* at Tchen-keou-tin in Sichuan. A dedicated missionary, he did magnificent work among the poor inhabitants of the area. During his time there he also discovered *A. sutchuenense* and *A. fargesii*, the latter being named after him by Rehder and later introduced into cultivation in 1902. *A. longipes* is another of his introductions.

Missionaries from other countries also played a part in the discovery of new *Acer* species. In Lo-fau-shan in the province of Kwantung, Dr Theol Faber, a member of the German Rhenish Missionary Society, discovered *A. fabri*, which Dr Hance named after him.

Russians

From another continent came a botanist and explorer whose collections were to be greater in both number and scientific importance: Carl Maximowicz. Born in Tula, Russia on November 11th 1827, he became an assistant of Professor Dr von Bunge at the botanical garden at St Petersburg and, in 1853, was sent out to the unexplored virgin forests of the Amur country and

Manchuria. He travelled there between 1854 and 1860 and then spent the next four years in Japan, proving himself to be a young and energetic botanical collector.

On July 10th 1864 he returned to St Petersburg with a rich collection of herbarium specimens, including many new plants. His collector Tschonoski was left behind in Japan and, until his death in 1887, he continued to look for plants. *A. tschonoskii* was named after him by Maximowicz. Among other maples found by Tschonoski are *A. capillipes* and *A. crataegifolium*, which he found in the province of Senaro, and also *A. cissifolium*.

As a collector and an author, Maximowicz was responsible for many other maples. He found *A. pseudosieboldianum* at Port Bruce, Vladivostock and *A. nikoense* (syn. *A. maximowiczianum*) in the province of Higo and Senaro in Japan. Other maples of which he is the author include *A. barbinerve* and *A. tegmentosum* from Manchuria, *A. argutum*, *A. capillipes*, *A. miyabei*, *A. mono* and *A. nikoense* from Japan, and *A. multiserratum* and *A. pilosum* from China. In Manchuria his collector Janowski found *A. mandschuricum* for him. Another of his collectors, Keisko, a Japanese botanist, found two maples at the volcano Wunsen: *A. rufinerve* and *A. sieboldianum*. In 1889 a maple found by Augustine Henry in Hubei, China was named *A. maximowiczii* by the German botanist Ferdinand Pax.

In 1874 the Russian Emperor Alexander II sent an expedition across Asia to China under the command of Captain Sosnovski. One of its members was Dr Pavel Jakovoevich Piasetski, an army surgeon and collector of natural objects. In June 1875, between the province of Shensi and Kansu, Piasetski found *A. discolor* and *A. pilosum*.

Another Russian, Grigori Nicolaevich Potanin, arrived with his wife in Beijing on January 3rd 1884, his expedition being financed by the Imperial Russian

Carl Maximowicz named *A. tschonoskii* after one of his tireless plant collectors.

Geographical Society. (During his second trip, when he visited Mount Omei, the journey proved too much for his wife, who fell ill and died. A fine species of rhubarb, *Rheum alexandrae*, is named after her.) Potanin discovered A. *multiserratum* on the River Lumbu on July 11th 1875, A. *betulifolium* (now known as A. *tetramerum* subsp. *betulifolium*) on Mount Idahoshan on July 15th 1885, and A. *urophyllum*, first at Moyping on July 4th 1875 and later the same month in Tshagon. A. *urophyllum* is now considered to be a subspecies of A. *maximowiczii*.

Further discoveries in Japan

Meanwhile, in Europe, further exploration of Japan was being planned. In 1877, the House of Veitch in London employed Charles Maries as a plant hunter. Maries was born at Stratford-upon-Avon and learned botany at Hampton Lucy where Rev John Stevens Henslow was headmaster. (Henslow was Professor of Botany at Cambridge and Charles Darwin was among his pupils.) He arrived in Japan on April 20th 1877. The object of his expedition was to collect seed of coniferous trees. In 1879, on the woody slopes surrounding Sapporo, he made a large collection of trees and shrubs, among which were many maples, including A. *crataegifolium*, A. *carpinifolium*, A. *rufinerve* and several varieties of A. *polymorphum* (syn. A. *palmatum*).

The next year, Maries collected A. *diabolicum*. The well-known gardener and traveller, Captain Collingwood Ingram, described this in his book *A Garden of Memories*: "... through a gap in the forest we espied a tree which seemed to be of a deep red colour. It formed a strikingly conspicuous object on the landscape, indeed an object that looked like the smouldering embers of a gigantic bonfire. The tree was covered with a multitude of small red flowers. The tree was A. *diabolicum* var. *purpurascens*."

Ingram was not correct to describe it as a variety, as it is in fact the male form of the species. In 1881 Maries introduced A. *nikoense* (syn. A. *maximowiczianum*) into cultivation.

In 1878 with Franchet, Paul Amedée Ludowic Savatier, a doctor in the French medical service, who lived in Japan between 1866 and 1875, published a maple he had collected. He named it A. *parviflorum*. However, this name was invalid because A. *parviflorum* Ehrh. (now a synonym of A. *spicatum*) had already been published. We now know Savatier's maple as A. *nipponicum*.

Charles Maries collected A. *rufinerve*, among other maples, in woods near Sapporo in 1879.

European maples

Although much plant-hunting activity was taking place in the East, there were also European maples being discovered at this time. In 1860 Friedrich Alexander Buhse, with Edmond Pierre Boissier, published an account of his journey to Transcaucasus and Persia. In the district of Talysch in the Eastern Caucasus he discovered A. *insigne* (now A. *velutinum*). In 1877 Dr M. T. Masters, Director of the Royal Botanic Gardens at Kew, received three plants from J. van Volxem, one each of A. *insigne*, A. *vanvolxemii* (now A. *velutinum* var. *vanvolxemii*) and A. *trautvetteri*. A. *vanvolxemii* was a tree little known in the wild. In the *Gardener's Chronicle* (1877) G. Nicholson related that seed was collected in the valley of the tributary of the Kura, above the military station of Lagodechi on the southern slopes of the central Caucasian chain. A. *insigne* was

PLATE II

A selection of maples

All leaves are shown at approximately half lifesize

also recorded by the German G. F. R. J. Radde in *Pflanzenwerb Kaukasusland* (1899) as growing in the valley of the Alasan river in the Central Caucasus.

In 1869 Karl Heinrich Emil Koch collected *A. quinquelobum* (*A. divergens*) in Tschorukthal in the basin of the Ryon river. This maple did not actually reach the Botanic Gardens at Kew until 1923.

Further discoveries in China

Now, the maples story returns to China, where, in 1887 Antwerp E. Pratt arrived. Although a professional plant hunter, Pratt was a leisurely traveller and near Tatsien-lu, among many other maples he saw and collected, he discovered *A. laxiflorum*.

The following year a remarkable Italian missionary, Father Giuseppe Giraldi, arrived in Shen-si. Giraldi had distinguished himself as a parish priest in North Italy before being posted to China, where he was to spend the rest of his life. Giraldi collected many maples and is responsible for introducing two: *A. giraldii*, which he found on Mount Taibai Shan in the province of Shen-si, and which was named after him by Pax; and *A. grosseri*, which he discovered in the mountains of Manghuansan, and which was not actually introduced into cultivation until many years later in 1919.

The Italian missionary, Father Guiseppe Giraldi, found *A. giraldii* on Mount Tabai Shan in China. It was named after him by the German botanist Ferdinand Pax.

Other collections made by Giraldi in the province of Shen-si included *A. erianthum* at Hua-tzo-pin, *A. caudatum* var. *multiserratum* at Taibai Shan, *A. maximowiczii* at Mount Lean-san, *A. oblongum* at Mount Huan-tou-san, *A. mono* and *A. robustum* at Qua-in-san, *A. tetramerum* var. *betulifolium* at several places including Shen-si and Kin-qua-san, and, at Kian-san, *Dipteronia sinensis*.

In 1881 Augustine Henry was appointed an inspector of customs in China. An Irishman, Henry had a keen interest in plants and was also a medical officer. He was to prove a fine and dedicated collector. In May 1885 he wrote to the Royal Botanic Gardens, Kew about the plants that he was seeing in China and he sent the gardens a multitude of specimens for identification. Henry was posted to Ichang, in the very heart of China. It was an area of great beauty and virgin forests which stretched for miles.

When his principal, Sir Robert Hart, gave him six months' leave in 1888, Henry travelled south-west into the districts of Chanyang, Patung and the southern part of Wushan before returning to Ichang. This was a trip of extraordinary interest during which Henry saw one tree of *Davidia involucrata*. He also collected two maples: *A. betulifolium* and *A. tenellum*.

Eight years later, in 1896, Henry made a trip to southern Yunnan, journeying to Meng-tse near the borders of French Indochina and to Szemao. During this time he found or discovered thirteen maples but then, depressed and tired after years of living and working under arduous conditions, he decided to return home. He wrote to Dr Thistleton Dyer, Director of Kew, that it would be worthwhile to send a collector to Ichang but, unfortunately, there were no funds available. Although the Arnold Arboretum in Boston, USA, which had been founded a few years previously, offered to fund Henry, he refused and returned home on December 31st 1900.

A form of A. *mono*, a species that was among a number of maples collected in China by Guiseppe Giraldi.

THE END OF THE NINETEENTH CENTURY

The nineteenth century closed with an interesting journey in Japan and the arrival in China of another famous plantsman. In 1892 Professor Charles Sprague Sargent, Director of the Arnold Arboretum, arrived in Japan. Although there had been an increasing American influence in the Far East since the mid-1850s, this was the first professional plant-hunting expedition sent out by America. Sargent had been appointed to the Arnold Arboretum a few years previously and was determined to increase the size and importance of its collections. In 1892 he introduced A. *capillipes* as a result of his travels in Japan. For some time he travelled with James Henry Veitch of the House of Veitch. On Mount Hakkoda, they spent an uncomfortable night together in a store hut in which neither the tall Veitch nor the burly Sargent could stand upright.

In 1895 Sargent collected A. *miyabei* and recorded the incident in his *Forest Flora of Japan*: "We stopped quite by accident at Iwanigawa railroad in Yezo, some forty or fifty miles from Sapporo and having a few minutes on our hands strolled out of the town to a tall grove of trees. In this grove occupying a piece of low ground on the borders of a small stream, we found *Acer pictum* and *Acer miyabei* covered in fruits. The find was a lucky one for Iwanigawa is a long way from the station where this maple had been discovered and mature fruit had not been seen before."

In the last year of the century the House of Veitch sent Ernest Henry Wilson to China. He was to become one of their greatest collectors. On arriving in China, Wilson set out to find the specimen of *Davidia involucrata* that Augustine Henry had found in 1888. Henry's instructions were so accurate that he found the tree without any problem but, unfortunately, it had been cut down to build a house.

For the next five years, Wilson travelled throughout China, collecting plants, and he was wonderfully successful in sending back thousands of specimens and seed. First, he explored the mountainous region of north-west Hupeh, which is rich in trees and shrubs. Then, he explored the limestone mountains of

Omeiwa and Wawu, another rich botanical area. On his return to England in 1905, Wilson found that the House of Veitch was on the verge of decline, but fortunately he was invited by the Arnold Arboretum to make another expedition to China, and during the next five years or so he made a number of expeditions, revisiting Omeiwa and Wawu and collecting plants for the Arnold Arboretum.

Wilson collected specimens and seeds of some thirty species and varieties of *Acer*. Among these were many new species, including *A. amplum*, *A. catalpifolium*, *A. ceriferum*, *A. erianthum*, *A. flabellatum*, *A. fulvescens*, *A. franchetii*, *A. henryi*, *A. laxiflorum*, *A. longipes*, *A. robustum*, *A. sinense*, *A. sutchuenense*, *A. wilsonii* and many others.

Writing of his journeys, Wilson said "Above Tungku the river makes a right-angled turn and is joined at this point by another stream of equal volume from the westward. From this place, the road skirts the river through a narrow savage magnificent wooded ravine and the maples *Acer davidii* and *Acer pictum* var. *parviflorum* are larger trees than I have seen elsewhere." He described the struggle for survival on Mount Omei. "The large-leafed cornel, *Cornus macrophylla*, manages to extend its area nearer to the base of the mountain being closely attended by several species of maple, amongst which *Acer davidii* with its white-striped bark is particularly prominent."

THE TWENTIETH CENTURY

It was in the early years of the twentieth century that the first expedition to be supported by a private patron took place. A syndicate led by Mr J. C. Williams of Caerhayes in Cornwall sent George Forrest to China.

Forrest had trained at the Edinburgh Botanic Gardens and was another intrepid traveller who spent many years in China making important collections. He arrived in China in the autumn of 1904 and soon got caught up with the uprisings that were taking place along the Chinese–Tibetan border. In one of these, he became encircled by insurgents and barely escaped with his life.

His principal place of exploration was the Likiang range of mountains, which are bounded by three great

Ernest Henry Wilson described seeing the eye-catching *A. davidii*, during travels on Mount Omei in China.

rivers, the Yang-tse, the Salween and the Mekong. He described this area as one huge natural flower garden. In 1905, on the eastern flank of the mountains, he found the maple that was subsequently named after him by Professor Diels, a German then working at the Royal Botanical Garden in Edinburgh.

Forrest also collected many other maples, including *A. amplum*, *A. campbellii*, *A. giraldii*, *A. laevigatum*, *A. oliverianum*, *A. paxii*, *A. taronense* and *A. tetramerum*, to mention a few.

Another private patron, Arthur Kilpin Bulley, a wealthy Liverpool cotton broker, financed Frank Kingdon-Ward, who arrived in Shanghai in 1907 to take up a teaching post. Most of his journeys took place outside China, in Assam, Burma and Tibet, as he was anxious not to cover territory that had been explored before. In 1914 in the Htawgaw Hills in Upper Burma, Kingdon-Ward discovered a maple that William Wright Smith named *A. wardii*, after him.

In *Plant Hunting on the Edge of the World* (1830) Kingdon-Ward wrote about this maple: "Welcome for their bright colouring are the maples. *Acer wardii* is a small rounded tree with three-pronged leaves, the prongs drawn out into long tails and the finely serrate margin bright red. It is abundant both in the Mishmi Hills and in the Seinghku valley, growing on the windy ridge with *Viburnum*, and *Ilex*, and *Rhododendron*. The hanging clusters of greenish flowers, produced in May, are followed in October by bunches of red wings; and the bright green leaves, beaded on the margin with red, are the first to colour in September, when they turn orange and scarlet. In the Mishmi Hills too is found *Acer campbellii*, a large tree with big palmate leaves and straw-coloured fruits, with purple stains on the widely divergent leaves. The most beautiful of the maples however is *Acer sikkimense*, more shrub than tree, and in Sikkim said to be always epiphytic. I saw only one plant in the Seinghku valley, alone on a bare ridge. Its simple polished leaves, borne on pillar-box red shoots, are quite unlike those of an ordinary maple, and the flowers open early. By May it is in fruit, long tassels of narrow red blades swinging from every shoot. In October these tassels, now six inches long, are still there, a dimmer red, nor have the leaves changed colour. *Acer sikkimense*, which grows about ten feet high, streaming with long ruby tails, composed of very small fruits, was one of the most gracious and ornamental shrubs I saw."

Other collectors at this time include William Purdom, who was born in Westmorland and received his horticultural training in the nurseries of Messrs Low and Sons and Messrs James Veitch & Co. Purdom arrived in China in 1909 and collected around Cho-ni. He introduced two maples: *A. stenolobum*, which he found in Shangii and *A. pilosum*, which he found on the road from Siku to Minchow in the province of Katsu.

Two Austrian botanists, Camillo Schneider and Handel Mazzetti, arrived in China at the end of 1913. They did a great deal towards helping us achieve a more complete knowledge of the flora of Yunna and south-west Sichuan. Handel Mazzetti discovered *A. taronense* in 1924 near the River Taron (Irriwaddy).

In about 1919, the Belgian-born Joseph Hers was appointed to the Chinese railway. When his work allowed it, he explored many forests in Honan, Kiangsu and other places. He discovered and introduced a number of woody plants, including a fine maple *A. hersii*, which Rehder named after him. (This is now considered to be a variety of *A. grosseri*.)

American expedition

An American expedition was organized at the end of 1928. It was accompanied by Herbert Stevens of Tring, one of the most recent serious collectors in China.

Two men from America, however, were also important: Frank N. Meyer and Joseph Rock. Meyer, a Dutchman, obtained a position in the US Department of Agriculture and was sent to eastern Asia to study and collect food plants. In 1907, he journeyed across Asia into China, exploring the area west of Tsingtaw, where he found and introduced *A. ginnala*. Joseph Rock, an Austrian who was professor of botany and Chinese at the University of Hawaii, was also employed by the Department of Agriculture. He was sent to China, Siam and Burma.

Rock was to spend many years in China, although he had to leave the country three times because of political troubles and travelling difficulties. In July 1929, in the valley of the Yalung river, Muli, Sichuan, he discovered *A. pentaphyllum*, a beautiful maple with digitate leaves. A few seeds of this germinated from his collection. One grew for a time in the nurseries of Hillier & Sons of Hampshire, but is no longer in existence. Another specimen is growing in the Strybing Arboretum, Golden Gate Park, San Francisco.

Chinese influence

By this time, the Chinese were beginning to recognize the importance of their own flora and, in the twentieth century, they introduced many new plants. *A. sinopurpurascens* was discovered by Cheng in 1931 and is in cultivation in Britain from seed sent to me from the Hang-zu Botanic Gardens in China. In 1939 Dr W. P. Fang wrote his *Monograph of Chinese Aceraceae*. He revised this in *Flora Republicae Popularis Sinicae* 1981, in which he describes many new species that are not yet in cultivation.

A number of expeditions to China in the last few years have resulted in the re-introduction of some maples as well as the discovery of some new ones.

Korea and Taiwan

Two other countries have so far had only a brief mention and their flora has only become relatively well-known in the last few decades: Korea and Taiwan.

Since the nineteenth century, when an expedition funded by the Royal Botanic Gardens, Kew, included among its number Richard Oldham, there have been very few expeditions to Korea. The country was visited in the 1890s by Admiral Schlippenbach, and he was followed by Komarov, who discovered *A. triflorum* in 1901, although this did not come into cultivation until 1923. Komarov also collected *A. barbinerve* and *A. tegmentosum*, which also grows in Manchuria, and *A. ukurunduense*, which is also found in Japan.

Lying about a hundred miles offshore from the mainland of South Korea in the Eastern Sea is a small volcanic island, Ullung-do. The island is dominated by an extinct volcano, Sari-bong, and contains a most important endemic flora, influenced by Japan. I visited the island in 1982, with members of the Royal Botanic Gardens, Kew, and was able to collect the two indigenous maples. These are *A. okamotoanum*, which is closely related to *A. mono*, and *A. takesimense*, which is closely related to *A. pseudosieboldianum*. The latter is a particularly fine maple, giving good autumn colour.

A number of beautiful maples are to be found growing in Taiwan (formerly Formosa). Richard Oldham, Charles Maries and Ernest H. Wilson all visited the island but none of them appear to have introduced many maples from there. However, there are some attractive indigenous species. At Trewithen, Cornwall, there is a fine specimen of *A. morrisonense* grown from seed collected by Yashiroda in 1932. In 1970 I entered into correspondence with Professor Huang of Taipei University and he was kind enough to collect and send seed of three species from Mount Morrison: *A. serrulatum*, *A. kawakamii* and *A. albopurpurascens*.

E. H. Wilson wrote in 1927: "The day of the plant hunter is finished and the world flora is almost an open book." Since that date there have been one world war and many regional wars, but due to advances in international diplomacy, travel in China and most other countries, is now possible. Perhaps the most intriguing destination for plant collectors, China is almost a continent rather than a country. It has an amazingly rich flora, and without doubt contains many plants that are yet to be found. Travel may now be easier and science more advanced, but courage and enterprise is still needed to discover plants in remote and distant places.

4

A CLASSIFICATION OF MAPLES

It has already been stated (p.11) that the genus *Acer* consists of not less than 120 species. The creation of the genus may be attributed to Joseph Pitton de Tournefort (1656–1708), who wrote about maples his book *Institutiones Rei Herbariae* (1700). In *Species Plantarum* (1753), Linnaeus described nine species, and in 1768 Philip Miller in the last edition of his famous *Gardeners' Dictionary* described ten species.

In 1885 Ferdinand Albin Pax identified 114 *Acer* species, which he divided into 13 sections. His monograph can be considered to be the earliest work of importance on the genus. The arrangement he proposed was accepted by Rehder in 1905, but it was criticized by Pojarkova in 1933.

The Chinese maples were studied by Dr W. P. Fang for over half a century. He wrote his first monograph in 1939, and in 1966 he published a second monograph in *Flora Reipublicae Popularis Sinicae* (1981 volume 46). In the latter monograph he described a number of new species and proposed a new section. Ken Ogata made a careful study of wood anatomy and morphology, the results of which he published in *A Systematic Study of the Genus Acer* (1967). He recognized 26 sections and abstained from subgeneric levels. Three years later, in his thesis *A Monograph of the Aceraceae* (1970), Murray proposed several new combinations.

A comprehensive study of flowering and sexual expression in the genus was published by Dr de Jong in 1976. This proposed a systematic scheme for the division of the genus *Acer*. He followed this in 1994 by proposing a new classification in *Maples of the World* (van Gelderen, de Jong and Oterdoom, Timber Press, 1994). The classification recognized 124 species in 16 sections, eight of which are further divided into 19 series. It is shown on the following pages.

It is not the purpose of this book, which is a guide to growing maples, to discuss Dr de Jong's classification. It is included here for those who wish to make a further study of the genus. It should be noted that taxonomy and classification are often a matter of debate and discussion, and that Dr de Jong has not always given reasons for his new names and combinations. Where I prefer a different name to that which he proposes, this is given in brackets in the following lists. In 'An A–Z of Species' (pp.53–115), the species concerned will be found under my preferred name.

New maples are being found all the time, and during the writing of this book, several new species have been discovered in China. This, along with new knowledge and new research, provides us with a constantly changing picture. For instance, it has recently been suggested that *A. mono* should now be called *A. pictum*.

ACER

Deciduous or evergreen trees, rarely shrubs; buds with several imbricate or two outer valvate scales; leaves opposite, petioled, simple or compound, usually palmately lobed or three to seven foliate; flowers usually andromonoecious or dioecious, 5-merous, rarely 4-merous, in racemes, panicles or corymbs, sepals sometimes connate, petals sometimes wanting, disk usually annular and large, rarely lobed or wanting, stamens 4–10 usually 8, styles or stigmas 2; fruits consisting of two long-winged compressed samaras (keys) joined together at the base.

A colourful form of *A. palmatum* in the autumn. This maple belongs to Section Palmata.

A. *distylum* belongs in Section Parviflora and has unusual lime-like leaves.

I Section Parviflora

1. Series Parviflora
   A. *nipponicum*

2. Series Distyla
   A. *distylum*

3. Series Caudata
   A. *caudatum* subsp. *caudatum*
   A. *caudatum* subsp. *multiserratum*
   A. *caudatum* subsp. *ukurunduense* (A. *ukuruduense*)
   A. *spicatum*

II Section Palmata

4. Series Palmata
   A. *ceriferum*
   A. *circinatum*
   A. *dupicatoserratum*
   A. *japonicum*
   A. *palmatum* subsp. *amoenum*
   A. *palmatum* subsp. *matsumurae*
   A. *palmatum* subsp. *palmatum*
   A. *pauciflorum*
   A. *pseudosieboldianum* subsp. *pseudosieboldianum*
   A. *pseudosieboldianum* subsp. *takesimense*
   A. *pubipalmatum*
   A. *robustum*
   A. *shirasawanum* var. *shirasawanum*
   A. *shirasawanum* var. *tenuifolium*
   A. *sieboldianum*

5. Series Sinensia
   A. *calcaratum*
   A. *campbellii* subsp. *campbellii*
   A. *campbellii* subsp. *chekiangense*
   A. *campbellii* subsp. *flabellatum* (A. *flabellatum*)
   A. *campbellii* subsp. *sinense* (A. *sinense*)
   A. *campbellii* subsp. *sinense* var. *longilobum*
   A. *campbellii* subsp. *wilsonii* (A. *wilsonii*)
   A. *chapaense*
   A. *confertifolium*
   A. *elegantulum*
   A. *erianthum*
   A. *fenzelianum*
   A. *kuomeii*
   A. *kweilinense*
   A. *lanpingense*
   A. *linganense*
   A. *mapienense*
   A. *miaoshanicum*
   A. *olivaceum*
   A. *oliverianum* subsp. *formosanum* (A. *serrulatum*)
   A. *oliverianum* subsp. *oliverianum*
   A. *schneiderianum*
   A. *shangszeense*
   A. *sichourense*
   A. *sunyiense*
   A. *taipuense*
   A. *tonkinense* subsp. *kwangsiense*
   A. *tonkinense* subsp. *liquidambarifolium*
   A. *tonkinense* subsp. *tonkinense*
   A. *tutcheri*
   A. *wuyuanense*
   A. *yaoshanicum*

A small tree with attractive bark and leaves, *A. capillipes* belongs to Section Macrantha.

6. Series Penninervia
   - A. *cordatum*
   - A. *crassum*
   - A. *erythranthum*
   - A. *eucalyptoides*
   - A. *fabri*
   - A. *hainanense*
   - A. *kiukiangense*
   - A. *laevigatum*
   - A. *lucidum*
   - A. *oligocarpum*
   - A. *sino-oblongum*
   - A. *yinkunii*

III Section Wardiana

- A. *wardii*

IV Section Macrantha

- A. *capillipes*
- A. *caudatifolium* (A. *kawakamii*)
- A. *crataegifolium*
- A. *davidii* subsp. *davidii*
- A. *davidii* subsp. *grosseri* (A. *grosseri*)
- A. *laisuense*
- A. *micranthum*
- A. *morifolium*
- A. *pectinatum* subsp. *forrestii* (A. *forrestii*)
- A. *pectinatum* subsp. *laxiflorum* (A. *laxiflorum*)
- A. *pectinatum* subsp. *maximowiczii* (A. *maximowiczii*)
- A. *pectinatum* subsp. *pectinatum*

A. *pectinatum* subsp. *taronense* (A. *taronense*)
A. *pensylvanicum*
A. *rubescens* (A. *morrisonense*)
A. *rufinerve*
A. *sikkimense* subsp. *metcalfii* (A. *metcalfii*)
A. *sikkimense* subsp. *sikkimense*
A. *tegmentosum*
A. *tschonoskii* subsp. *tschonoskii*
A. *tschonoskii* subsp. *koreanum*

V Section Glabra

7. Series Glabra
A. *glabrum* subsp. *diffusum*
A. *glabrum* subsp. *douglasii*
A. *glabrum* subsp. *glabrum*
A. *glabrum* subsp. *neomexicanum*
A. *glabrum* subsp. *siskiyouense*

8. Series Arguta
A. *acuminatum*
A. *argutum*
A. *barbinerve*
A. *stachyophyllum* subsp. *betulifolium*
A. *stachyophyllum* subsp. *stachyophyllum* (A. *tetramerum*)

VI Section Negundo

9. Series Negundo
A. *negundo* subsp. *californicum*
A. *negundo* subsp. *interius*
A. *negundo* subsp. *mexicanum*
A. *negundo* subsp. *negundo*

10. Series Cissifolia
A. *cissifolium*
A. *henryi*

VII Section Indivisa

A. *carpinifolium*

VIII Section Acer

11. Series Acer
A. *caesium* subsp. *caesium*
A. *caesium* subsp. *giraldii* (A. *giraldii*)

The colourful autumn leaves of A. *cissifolium*, which belongs to Section Negundo.

- A. *heldreichii* subsp. *heldreichii*
- A. *heldreichii* subsp. *trautvetteri* (A. *trautvetteri*)
- A. *pseudoplatanus*
- A. *velutinum*

12. Series Monspessulana
- A. *hyrcanum* subsp. *hyrcanum*
- A. *hyrcanum* subsp. *intermedium*
- A. *hyrcanum* subsp. *keckianum*
- A. *hyrcanum* subsp. *reginae-amaliae*
- A. *hyrcanum* subsp. *sphaerocarpum*
- A. *hyrcanum* subsp. *stevenii*
- A. *hyrcanum* subsp. *tauricolum*
- A. *monspessulanum* subsp. *assyriacum*
- A. *monspessulanum* subsp. *cinerascens*
- A. *monspessulanum* subsp. *ibericum*
- A. *monspessulanum* subsp. *microphyllum*
- A. *monspessulanum* subsp. *monspessulanum*
- A. *monspessulanum* subsp. *oksalianum*
- A. *monspessulanum* subsp. *persicum*
- A. *monspessulanum* subsp. *turcomanicum*
- A. *obtusifolium*
- A. *opalus* subsp. *hispanicum* (A. *granatense*)
- A. *opalus* subsp. *obtusatum*
- A. *opalus* subsp. *opalus*
- A. *sempervirens*

13. Series Saccharodendron
- A. *saccharum* subsp. *floridanum*
- A. *saccharum* subsp. *grandidentatum* (A. *grandidentatum*)
- A. *saccharum* subsp. *leucoderme* (A. *leucoderme*)
- A. *saccharum* subsp. *nigrum* (A. *nigrum*)
- A. *saccharum* subsp. *ozarkense*
- A. *saccharum* subsp. *saccharum*
- A. *saccharum* subsp. *skutchii*
- A. *saccharum* var. *rugelii*
- A. *saccharum* var. *schneckii*
- A. *saccharum* var. *sinuosum*

IX Section Pentaphylla

14. Series Pentaphylla
- A. *pentaphyllum*

15. Series Trifida
- A. *buergerianum* subsp. *buergerianum*
- A. *buergerianum* subsp. *formosanum*
- A. *buergerianum* subsp. *ningpoense*
- A. *coriaceifolium*
- A. *discolor*
- A. *fengii*
- A. *oblongum*
- A. *paxii*
- A. *shihweii*
- A. *sycopseoides*
- A. *wangchii* subsp. *tsinyunense*
- A. *wangchii* subsp. *wangchii*
- A. *yui*

X Section Trifoliata

16. Series Grisea
- A. *griseum*
- A. *maximowiczianum* (A. *nikoense*)
- A. *triflorum*

17. Series Mandshurica
- A. *mandshuricum*
- A. *sutchuenense*

XI Section Lithocarpa

18. Series Lithocarpa
- A. *diabolicum*
- A. *leipoense*
- A. *sinopurpurascens*
- A. *sterculiaceum* subsp. *franchetii* (A. *franchetii*)
- A. *sterculiaceum* subsp. *sterculiaceum* (A. *villosum*)
- A. *sterculiaceum* subsp. *thomsonii* (A. *thomsonii*)

19. Series Macrophylla
- A. *macrophyllum*

XII Section Platanoidea

- A. *campestre*
- A. *cappadocicum* subsp. *cappadocicum*
- A. *cappadocicum* subsp. *divergens* (A. *divergens*)
- A. *cappadocicum* subsp. *lobelii* (A. *lobelii*)
- A. *cappadocicum* subsp. *sinicum*
- A. *cappadocicum* subsp. *sinicum* var. *tricaudatum*
- A. *longipes* subsp. *amplum* (A. *amplum*)
- A. *longipes* subsp. *catalpifolium* (A. *catalpifolium*)
- A. *longipes* subsp. *firmianioides*

A. *saccharinum* 'Laciniatum Weiri' has more deeply dissected leaves than the species, which belongs in Section Ginnala.

A. *longipes* subsp. *longipes* (A. *fulvescens*)
A. *miyabei* subsp. *maiotaiense*
A. *miyabei* subsp. *miyabei*
A. *mono* subsp. *mono*
A. *mono* subsp. *mono* f. *ambiguum*
A. *mono* subsp. *okamotoanum* (A. *okamotoanum*)
A. *mono* var. *mayrii*
A. *nayongense*
A. *platanoides* subsp. *platanoides*
A. *platanoides* subsp. *turkestanicum* (A. *turkestanicum*)
A. *tenellum*
A. *tibetense*
A. *truncatum*

XIII Section Pubescentia

A. *pentapomicum*
A. *pilosum*

XIV Section Ginnala

A. *tataricum* subsp. *aidzuense*
A. *tataricum* subsp. *ginnala* (A. *ginnala*)
A. *tataricum* subsp. *semenovii*
A. *tataricum* subsp. *tataricum*

XV Section Rubra

A. *pycnanthum*
A. *rubrum*
A. *saccharinum*

XVI Section Hyptiocarpa

A. *garrettii*
A. *laurinum*

5

AN A–Z OF SPECIES

A wide range of the species, subspecies, varieties and cultivars of the genus *Acer* are described in this chapter. While the list is not exhaustive, it is intended as a representative selection.

In describing these plants, I have used the names with which I am most comfortable. These are those that came into general use after the work of Ferdinand Pax (1902) but before the latest survey and research into the genus carried out by Dr P. C. de Jong. However, for clarity, where the names differ, those proposed by Dr de Jong are given in brackets.

In the A–Z, each maple is given a full description so that it could be identified if it were encountered, but botanical terms have been avoided wherever possible. Where they have been used, they are defined in the glossary in the appendices (p.151).

The eventual height of each maple is provided, along with details of the bark and the buds. Buds are an important aid to identification. An unusual feature in maples is that some species, such as *A. davidii*, have stalked buds. This feature is also found in the genus *Alnus* (alder). A detailed description of the leaves is also given, including the shape of the lobes and the character of the sinuses (the space between the lobes) and the margins. Where hairs are found on the leaves these are described, too, as they can be important.

The appearance of the flowers and the fruit is also covered, including, in many cases, the angle of the wings (see p.17), which can also help identification. Where fruit length is given, it is the combined length of the nutlet and wing.

A small to medium-sized tree, *A. caesium* has leaves with long, bright red stalks.

Acer acuminatum
Wall. ex D. Don

A deciduous, small tree, to 12m (40ft) high, producing purplish branches that later become green with white lenticels. The buds are crimson and pointed with a few scales. Bright glossy green leaves, 9–12cm (3½–5in) long, have 3–5 triangular lobes, which are prolonged at the tip into tail-like points that can be strikingly long and slender and the margins are sharply toothed, sometimes doubly so. The leaf undersides are lighter green with some hairs in the nerve axils. The leaves are attractively tinted in autumn. Yellowish-green flowers are borne in terminal raceme-like panicles and are andromonoecious. The simple lax racemes of fruits are 10–18cm (4–7in) long, the wings spreading at right angles and, with the nutlet, being 2–2.5cm (¾–1in) long. Grows in all soils. Himalayas. Introduced c1845.

Acer albopurpurascens
Hayata

An evergreen, small tree, to 11m (35ft) high, with light grey bark and brownish buds. The leaves, 7–12cm (3–5in) long, are leathery and oblong-lanceolate, coming to a point at the apex and rounded at the base; they are pale green and hairless above, glaucous beneath. The fruit, 2–2.5cm (¾–1in) long, are carried in cymes; they have small, smooth nutlets and the wings spread at obtuse angles. A tender maple, grown mainly by collectors. Taiwan. Introduced 1978.

Acer amplum
Rehder (*A. longipes* subsp. *amplum* (Rehder) P. C. de Jong)

A deciduous, small tree, to 11m (35ft) high, with green

A. buergerianum has distinctive three-lobed leaves of a dark and glossy green.

branches that become light grey with age and purplish-brown buds. The leaves, 10–18cm (4–7in) across, are usually 5-lobed, the lobes broad-ovate, wider than long, and coming to an abrupt point. They are smooth and light green above, lighter beneath with some hairs in the axil of the veins. Andromonoecious flowers are borne in loose terminal corymbs. The fruits are purplish at first then yellowish-brown, the nutlets with wings are 3.5–5cm (1½–2in) long and spreading at a wide angle. China. Introduced 1908.

Acer argutum
Maxim.

A deciduous, small, upright tree, to 11m (35ft) high, with purplish branches becoming greyish-brown with age. The leaves are 5–10cm (2–4in) long and as much wide, with five ovate and pointed lobes and attractively double-toothed margins. They are deep green and smooth above, paler underneath and softly hairy. The veins are elevated beneath and impressed minutely above. Greenish-yellow flowers are carried in terminal racemes and are followed by fruits about 2.5cm (1in) long with the wings spreading at about 180 degrees. Japan. Introduced 1881.

Acer barbinerve
Maxim.

A deciduous, small tree, to 11m (35ft) high, often multi-branched. The young branches are bright crimson, becoming greyish with age, and the reddish buds are sharp-pointed and have long, weak hairs (villous). The rounded leaves, with heart-shaped bases and coarsely toothed margins, are deep green above, lighter underneath with some brown hairs. They are 5-lobed with two small basal lobes with a narrow space between them. The flowers are yellowish, the males in short clusters, the females on a raceme. The fruits are 1cm (½in) long, the wings spreading at an angle of about 120 degrees. This is an attractive maple that grows in woodland conditions and prefers a soil that is not too alkaline. Korea, Manchuria. Introduced about 1890.

Acer buergerianum

Miq. Trident maple

A deciduous, small to medium-sized tree, up to 14m (45ft) high, with greyish bark and small, brown buds. Dark glossy green leaves, 4–9cm (1½–3½in) long, have have three distinct triangular lobes with margins that are untoothed or nearly so. The undersides of the leaves are lighter, smooth and slightly glaucous. Small flowers are produced in corymbs; the fruits are 2–2.5cm (¾–1in) long and the wings are almost parallel. This tree has attractive tints of scarlet and yellow in autumn. China, Japan, Korea, Taiwan. Introduced about 1890.

'Maruba Tokaede' ('Integrifolium') The leaves are more leathery and not as deeply lobed; the side lobes are short and blunt and are near the apex of the leaf.

'Miyasama Yatsubusa' The leaves are small with prominent side lobes. They are reddish when unfolding in spring. A delightful dwarf with short, stubby growth.

'Naruto Kaede' The leaves are deep rich green with three triangular lobes – the centre one longer than the lateral ones, producing a T-shape. The margins roll inward. A most attractive and unusual shrubby form with good autumn colour.

Acer caesium

Wall. ex Brandis

A deciduous, small to medium-sized tree, up to 14m (45ft) high, with greyish bark and large, pointed, ash-grey or light brown buds that have many scales. The large leaves, 18–22cm (7–9in) long and 22–30cm (9–12in) wide, are 5-lobed, the lobes being broad-ovate and coming to a point, with slightly toothed margins. Browny-bronze when unfolding in spring, they later become green and smooth. They have long red stalks. Yellowish-green flowers are borne in short racemes, followed by fruits, 5cm (2in) long, which spread at right angles. Grows in all soils. Himalayas, south-west China. Introduced *c*1800.

Acer calcaratum

Gagne. (*A. craibianum* Delendick)

A deciduous, small tree, to 10m (30ft) high, with bark that is green at first, later light brown; the buds are reddish-brown. Dark green leaves have three tapered pointed lobes, with wide sinuses; the central lobe is longer than the lateral lobes. They are rounded at the base with untoothed margins. The lower surface is dull green and prominently veined. The greenish-yellow flowers are followed by fruits, 2.5–3.5cm (1–1½in) long, that spread at a wide angle. A rare, tender maple. Burma (now Myanmar), Thailand. Introduced *c*1987.

Acer campbellii

Hook. f. & Thoms. ex Hiern.

A deciduous, medium-sized tree, to 18m (60ft) high, smaller in cultivation. The green branchlets have some bloom and later become light brown, and the winter buds are small and green with a touch of purplish-red at the tip. The leaves, 8–12cm (3–5in) long, have 5–7 broad-ovate lobes coming to a tail-like point and with sharply toothed margins. They are bright green above, lighter underneath with hairs in the vein axils, especially when young; the stalks are red. Flowers are borne in terminal panicles; the sepals yellowish, the petals white. Smooth fruits, 3.5–5cm (1½–2in) long, spread almost horizontally. A tender maple. Himalayas, Upper Burma, Vietnam. Introduced about 1851.

The tree examined at the Sir Harold Hillier Gardens and Arboretum had two buds at the end of the branch, one large and one small.

var. yunnanense Rehder (*A. campbellii* subsp. *flabellatum* var. *yunnanense*) has leaves with 3–5 sharply toothed lobes and red stalks.

Acer campestre

L. Field maple

A deciduous, medium-sized tree, to 15m (50ft) high, with light greenish-brown bark, which is sometimes corky, and brown winter buds. The leaves, 5–7cm (2–3in) across, have 3–5 lobes, rounded at the tips and with untoothed margins. They are reddish-brown in spring, maturing dull green above, lighter beneath and downy, and are yellow or sometimes red in autumn. When the leaf stalks are broken, they exude a milky juice. Small, green flowers are produced in small corymbs. The fruits, 2.5cm (1in) or more long, spread horizontally and are usually softly hairy. Grows in all soils. Europe, west Asia, North Africa.

'Carnival' The leaves are attractively variegated. They are green, edged with pink and white.

'Postelense' Leaves golden-yellow when young.

A. *capillipes* has 3- to 5-lobed leaves that turn brilliant scarlet in autumn, and attractive bark with white markings.

'Pulverulentum' Leaves are blotched with white speckles.

'Royal Ruby' The leaves are purple, especially when they are young in the spring but usually lasting through summer.

'Schwerinii' Leaves are purple when young, afterwards turning green.

Acer capillipes
Maxim.

A deciduous, small tree, to 10m (30ft) high, with attractive purplish-red bark that has white striations, later becoming greenish or grey-green. The buds are reddish-purple and stalked. The leaves, 7–12cm (3–5in) long, are red when unfolding in spring and brilliant bright scarlet in autumn. They are heart-shaped at the base and have three, or rarely five, triangular lobes; the central lobe is larger than the side lobes and terminates with a tapering point. The margins are doubly toothed. Greenish-white flowers are borne in drooping slender racemes. Spreading at an obtuse angle or nearly horizontally, the fruits are 1–2cm (½–¾in) long. Grows on most soils but prefers one that is not too alkaline. Japan. Introduced 1892.

Acer cappadocicum
Gled.

A deciduous, medium-sized to large tree, to 20m (65ft) high, with branchlets that are bloomy when young, green in the second year, and mature light grey. The rounded buds are reddish-purple and bloomy. Leaves, 7–15cm (3–6in) across, have 5–7 lobes and heart-shaped bases. The lobes are triangular-ovate with long, tapering tips and untoothed margins. The leaves are bright green above, lighter green beneath with prominent veins and some tufts of hairs in the axil of the veins. They turn attractive tints of yellow in autumn. When broken, the stalks exude a milky sap. Yellow flowers are carried in corymbs and are followed by fruits with wings 3–4.5cm (1¼–1¾in) long and spreading at a wide angle. Caucasus, North Turkey and Iran. Introduced 1838.

'Aureum' A small tree, to 14m (45ft) high, growing more slowly. The leaves are reddish-purple in spring, becoming yellow and later a greenish-yellow.

'Rubrum' Young leaves are blood-red when unfolding in spring, later becoming green.

The ivy-like, bright green leaves of *A. cappadocicum* have tapering tips and untoothed margins.

subsp. sinicum (Rehder) Hand.-Mazz. Buds are reddish-purple and short with about five scales. Leaves are bright green above, lighter beneath, and are smaller than the type. They have five lobes with wide sinuses and long tapering points each with a pendent tip. The margins are untoothed and the stalks red. Yellow flowers are borne in corymbs followed by remarkable bright red fruits. Himalayas, China. Introduced 1901.

Acer carpinifolium

Siebold & Zucc. Hornbeam maple

A deciduous, small tree, to 10m (30ft) high, with smooth, dark greyish bark and light brownish-green, many-scaled buds. Oblong leaves, 7–10cm (3–4in) long and 5cm (2in) or so wide, have double-toothed margins and are dark green above, lighter underneath with about 20 parallel veins, densely covered with grey silky hairs when young, later becoming hairless. They turn attractive tints of yellow in autumn. They do not fall immediately, but later in winter or early spring (marcescent). Green flowers are usually in racemes on a longer, slender stalk. Fruits, about 1cm (½in) long, have wings curved in the shape of a bow. Grows on most soils but prefers one that is about neutral. Japan. Introduced 1879.

Acer catalpifolium

Rehder (*A. longipes* subsp. *catalpifolium* (Rehder) P. C. de Jong)

A deciduous, large tree, to 30m (100ft) in the wild, probably smaller in cultivation. The branchlets are green or purplish-green, becoming dark grey or brownish-grey, and have reddish buds. The thin leaves are 10–20cm (4–8in) long and ovate or ovate-oblong, with tapering tips, and entire or occasionally with undeveloped lateral lobes below the middle. The upper surface is deep green and hairless, the lower surface is pale green with tufts of hair at the base of the nerves. Greenish-yellow flowers are carried in terminal

PLATE III

A selection of green-leaved maple species

All leaves are shown at approximately half lifesize

In the autumn *A. cissifolium* produces long racemes of nutlets with wings spreading at a narrow angle.

corymbs. Yellowish fruits, 4–5cm (1½–2in) long, spread at right angles. A very rare and rather tender maple. China. Introduced 1992.

Acer caudatum

Wall. (*A. papilio* King)

A deciduous, medium-sized tree, to 15m (50ft) or more in the wild, smaller in cultivation, with ash-grey, roughish bark. The leaves are 7–12cm (3–5in) long and about as wide. They have five lobes and are heart-shaped at the base. The lobes are ovate, coming to a sharp point at the tip, with sharply saw-toothed margins. The upper surface is bright green, the lower surface has yellowish-brown hairs. Flowers in spike-like panicles are followed by greenish fruit, 2.5cm (1in) or so long, spreading at an acute angle. West Himalayas and Upper Burma. Introduced before 1910.

Acer cinnamomifolium

Hayata (*A. coriaceifolium* Lèv.)

An evergreen, small tree, to 10m (30ft) high, with pale grey bark and light brownish buds. The bright apple-green leaves, 6–10cm (2½–4in) long, are leathery and oblong without lobes or teeth. The leaf underside is paler than the upper surface. Greenish-white flowers are borne in corymbs and are followed by fruits, 2.5–3.5cm (1–1½in) long, that spread at an acute angle. A rare tender maple. China. Introduced 1982.

Acer circinatum

Pursh Vine maple

A deciduous, large shrub or small tree, up to 10m (30ft) high, with smooth, light grey bark and reddish-purple buds. Bright green leaves, 7–12cm (3–5in) wide, are roundish with 7–9 small, ovate lobes that have narrow sinuses and terminate with a point. The leaf bases are heart-shaped and the margins doubly toothed. The undersides are pale with some hairs when young. They have attractive autumn tints of scarlet and orange. Flowers, in small corymbs, have reddish-purple tepals and white petals. Fruits, 3.5cm (1½in) long, spread almost horizontally. Western United States and south-west Canada. Introduced 1826.

'Little Gem' A small shrub that grows to 1m (3ft) and is densely branched.

'Monroe' Large shrub, to 4m (12ft) high, with 5–7-lobed leaves, deeply cut to the base.

Acer cissifolium

(Siebold & Zucc.) K. Koch

A deciduous, small, rounded tree, to 10m (30ft) high. Downy at first, the branchlets become light grey and smooth. The buds are reddish-purple or dark purple and long pointed. Leaves consist of three leaflets carried on a slender common stalk. They are bright green above, paler beneath and smooth, except for some hairs in the axil of the veins. Each leaflet is 5–7cm (2–3in) long and terminates in a short, blunt point. The leaf margins are coarsely and irregularly toothed, especially towards the tip. Small flowers, with yellow petals, are borne in long racemes. The fruit are also borne in long racemes and are 2.5cm (1in) long, the wings spreading at an angle of six degrees or less. This is a graceful maple with autumn tints of red and yellow. Grows in all soils. Japan. Introduced before 1870.

Acer × conspicuum (*A. davidii* × *A. pensylvanicum*)

Van Gelderen et Oterdoom

This deciduous maple grows to about 8–10m (25–30ft) tall and has triangular leaves, 5–20cm (2–8in) long with 3–5 short-tapering lobes. Several cultivars have been named. Their most stiking feature is their beautiful striped bark.

'Elephant's Ear' Purple bark with white stripes.

'Phoenix' Bright red young stems.

'Silver Cardinal' Variegated foliage when young, and bright red young stems.

'Silver Vein' Blue-green bark, striped with white, and leaves with 3 lobes.

Acer cordatum

Pax

A semi-evergreen, small tree, to 10m (30ft) high, with smooth, grey bark. The oblong, unlobed leaves, 6–11cm (2½–4½in) long, are rounded at the base and have untoothed margins. They are brownish-green and smooth on both surfaces. Flowers are borne in small corymbs. They are followed by fruits, 2.5cm (1in) or so long, spreading at an obtuse angle or nearly horizontally. A very rare maple. China. Introduced 1983.

Acer crataegifolium

Siebold & Zucc. Hawthorn maple

A deciduous, small tree, to 10m (30ft) high, producing purplish branchlets with white striations, becoming darker with age. The buds are small, purple and stalked. The oval leaves, 5–7cm (2–3in) long, are usually unlobed although they may have 3–5 shallow lobes. They taper to a long point and have heart-shaped bases and coarsely toothed, wavy margins. Reddish-violet when unfolding in spring, they mature to bright green above, paler beneath with some hairs in the axils of the veins, and have attractive autumn tints. Erect racemes of yellowish-white flowers are produced in mid-spring along with the young leaves. The fruits are smooth and have rose-red wings, 2–2.5cm (¾–1in) long, that spread at nearly 180 degrees. Japan. Introduced 1879.

Acer davidii

Franch.

A deciduous, small to medium-sized tree, to 10–15m (30–50ft) high, but often a little less in cultivation. It has green or purplish-red bark striped with white, darkening with age, and small, purple and stalked buds. The dark glossy green leaves are ovate to ovate-oblong, with a tapering tip and a heart-shaped or rounded base. The margins are saw-toothed or slightly scalloped. The lower surface of the leaves is pale green with some reddish hairs on the veins when young. The veins are prominent and radiate from a bridge at the base of the stalk. Small, greenish-yellow flowers are produced in long racemes. The female flowers have stalks and are borne in longer racemes than the males. Abundant brownish-green or brownish-yellow fruits are also produced in racemes; the nutlets have wings 2.5–4cm (1–1½in) long, spreading at an obtuse angle. China. Introduced 1879.

Although the leaves of *A. davidii* are normally unlobed, there are forms that have small lobes near the base; also 3-lobed leaves predominate on young trees.

The species has a wide range in China. Charles Maries introduced it from the Ichang area of West Hubei for Veitch in 1879 and Wilson collected seed in the same locality in 1902. The plant they found has a compact habit with the branches having short internodes and the leaves being up to 10–12cm (4–5in) long. Forrest collected *A. davidii* in Yunnan and his form has a looser open habit, longer internodes of up to 10cm (4in), and larger leaves, up to 19cm (7½in) long. Forrest's plant is also distinct in having purplish young stems.

In China, a number of collections have been made in recent years; these are in cultivation under several collector's numbers. Some seedlings have also been selected and are named. For example, **'Madeleine Spitta'**, which was raised at Winkworth Arboretum, Surrey, and is upright in habit, and **'Serpentine'**, which has purplish bark, striped with white.

Acer diabolicum

K. Koch Horned maple

A deciduous, small tree, to about 10m (30ft) high. When the branchlets are young, they are covered with whitish hairs, later becoming greyish and smooth. The large, dark brown buds have many scales. The leaves, 10–18cm (4–7in) wide, are heart-shaped at the base and have five broad-ovate lobes that come to a short, tapering point. They are dark green above, paler beneath, covered with whitish hairs on both surfaces when young, later only sparingly underneath. They turn purplish in autumn. Male and female flowers are borne on separate trees; they are yellow and the males have red stamens. They appear in short, pendent corymbs in mid-spring, before the leaves. The nutlets are covered with numerous whitish, stinging bristles; the wings are 4–4.5cm (1½–1¾in) long and usually

A. distylum is a rare species with bright green unlobed leaves that turn yellow in autumn.

parallel. This is an attractive maple, although rare in cultivation. Japan. Introduced 1880.

f. purpurascens This is a name often wrongly given to the male form with flowers with bright red sepals.

Acer distylum

Siebold & Zucc.

A deciduous, medium-sized tree, to 15m (50ft) high, although often smaller in cultivation. The branches are reddish-orange when young, becoming reddish-brown, and the buds are brownish, the two outer scales covering the inner ones. The leaves, 10–16.5cm (4–6½in) long, are ovate without lobes and come to a long, slender point at the apex. Heart-shaped at the base with finely toothed margins, they are bright green above, paler beneath with some hairs when young but later smooth. Yellowish flowers are produced in upright terminal racemes. They are followed by smooth fruits in erect racemes; the wings are 3cm (1¼in) long and spread at an angle of about 100 degrees. An unusual, rare maple. Japan. Introduced 1879.

Acer divergens

Pax (*A. cappadocicum* subsp. *divergens* (Pax) A. E. Murray)

A deciduous, small tree, to 10m (30ft) high, with greyish bark and greenish-red, rounded buds. The bright green leaves are 2.5–6cm (1–2½in) wide with 3–5 lobes, which are broad-ovate and abruptly taper-pointed. The leaf undersides are paler than their upper surfaces. Corymbs of yellow flowers are followed by reddish-brown fruit, about 2.5cm (1in) long, which spread at a wide angle. A pretty maple, rare in cultivation. Transcaucasus and Turkey. Introduced 1923.

Acer elegantulum

W. P. Fang & L. C. Chiu

A deciduous, small tree, to 10m (30ft) high, with green bark covered with lenticels, and small, reddish-purple, pointed buds. The papery, 5-lobed leaves are 6–10cm (2½–4in) across with truncate bases. They are bright green above and paler beneath with some white hairs in the vein axils. The lobes are ovate and have long, tapering points, except for the two smaller basal lobes, which are small and ovate-lanceolate. Flowers are borne in terminal drooping racemes. They are yellowish with red petals. Small fruits, 1–2cm (½–¾in) long, with smooth nutlets, spread almost horizontally. A most attractive maple. China. Introduced 1982.

Acer erianthum

Schwer.

A deciduous, small tree, to 10m (30ft) high. The young branchlets are greenish, turning greenish-grey when mature, and the buds are small. The leaves have dark green upper surfaces and paler undersides with conspicuous tufts of white hairs in the vein axils. They are papery, 5–11cm (2–4½in) long and have 5–7 ovate lobes, with short, tapering tips and deep sinuses. Heart-shaped at the base, they have sharply and unevenly toothed margins. Terminal panicles of yellowish flowers are followed by yellowish-purple fruits, with strongly convex nuts and wings, 6–7cm (2½–3in) long, that spread horizontally. China. Introduced 1907.

Acer fabri

Hance

An evergreen or semi-evergreen, small tree, to 10m (30ft) high, with bright reddish-purple bark, later brownish-grey, and reddish buds. The leathery leaves, 7–12cm (3–5in) long, are oblong or oblong-lanceolate, unlobed, pointed at the tip and rounded at the base. The upper surface is deep green and smooth, the lower surface is paler with some hairs. Flowers are borne in panicles and have purplish-white petals. Brownish-yellow fruits, up to 3.5cm (1½in) long, spread at an obtuse angle. This species is particularly notable in spring for its attractive reddish foliage. A little tender. East Himalayas, China. Introduced 1884.

Acer flabellatum

Rehder (A. *campbellii* subsp. *flabellatum* (Rehder) E. Murray)

A deciduous, small tree, to 10m (30ft) high, less in cultivation. The smooth branches are green at first, later becoming greenish-brown. The buds are brownish and hairy. Rounded, sharply toothed leaves are 7–12cm (3–5in) in diameter and usually 7-lobed. The lobes are ovate or ovate-oblong and taper-pointed. The upper surface is deep green, the lower surface paler green with tufts of white hairs in the axils. Greenish flowers, with white petals, are borne in panicles. They are followed by yellowish-brown fruits, 3.5–5cm (1½–2in) long and spreading horizontally. An attractive maple, but a little tender. China. Introduced 1907.

Acer forrestii

Diels (A. *pectinatum* subsp. *forrestii* (Diels) E. Murray)

A deciduous, small tree, to 11m (35ft) high, producing purple or reddish-purple branchlets with white stripes that become greyish-brown. The buds are small, purple and stalked. Papery leaves, 5–11cm (2–4½in) long, are heart-shaped at the base with red stalks and have 3–5 triangular, taper-pointed lobes, the central lobe longer than the side lobes. The margins are finely toothed. The upper surface is deep glossy green while the lower surface is pale green with tufts of brown hairs in the axils of the veins. Yellowish-green flowers are borne in slender racemes. Smooth fruits, 2–2.5cm (¾–1in) wide, spread almost horizontally. A graceful maple that is not tolerant of chalk soils. Sichuan, Sikang and Yunnan in central and south-west China. Introduced 1906.

'Alice' Leaves are attractively marked with pink, but not always dependable. The leaf shape is not typical of A. *forrestii*, and it is probably a hybrid with A. *davidii*.

Acer franchetii

Pax (A. *sterculiaceum* subsp. *franchetii* (Pax) E. Murray)

A deciduous, small tree, to 11m (35ft) high, with dark brown bark and dark brown winter buds with numerous scales. The leaves are 7–15cm (3–6in) long and papery with heart-shaped bases. They have 3–5 triangular lobes that are forward-pointing, taper-pointed and have remotely toothed margins. Their upper surface is deep green, while the lower surface is paler with tufts of hair at the axils of the veins. Flowers are yellowish-green and carried on slender racemes. Fruits, with slightly hairy nutlets, are yellowish-brown, 3.5–5cm (1½–2in) long and spread at right angles. An attractive maple. China. Introduced 1901.

A. *forrestii* is an interesting small tree with reddish-purple branches and red-stalked leaves.

A young specimen of A. *giraldii*, which is a rare species that will eventually make an open-crowned tree.

Acer × freemanii

Murray (A. *rubrum* × A. *saccharinum*)

A deciduous tree growing to 15m (50ft) or so tall. The leaves are intermediate between the two parents, being not as deeply lobed as A. *saccharinum*, but more cut than A. *rubrum*, with rounded to acute sinuses.

A number of good cultivars have been produced and are particularly notable for their autumn colours. They include **'Armstrong'** (upright in habit), **'Autumn Blaze'**, **'Autumn Fantasy'** (brilliant spring flowers), **'Celebration'**, **'Marmo'** (attractive spring flowers) and **'Scarlet Sentinel'** (upright habit with brilliant spring flowers).

Acer fulvescens

Rehder

A deciduous, small tree, to about 11m (35ft) high, with grey or yellowish-grey, slightly fissured bark and large, brownish, blunt-pointed buds. The wavy-edged, papery, dark green leaves, 10–11cm (4–4½in) long, are usually 3-lobed but sometimes have two additional basal lobes. The lobes are short and triangular, each with a long tail-like point; the tip of the central lobe curls over. They have wide sinuses. The lower surface is pale green with brown hairs along the veins. Yellowish flowers are carried in panicles and are followed by yellowish fruit, 2–2.5cm (¾–1in) long, spreading nearly horizontally. China. Introduced 1908.

Acer ginnala

Maxim. (A. *tataricum* subsp. *ginnala* (Maxim.) Wesm.)

A deciduous, small tree or large, bushy shrub, to 6m (20ft) high, with rough, grey bark and small, dark reddish-brown buds. The leaves are papery, 6–7cm (2½–3in) long and heart-shaped at the base. They are triangular and 3-lobed when young, later the lobes become quite shallow; the central lobe is much longer than the side lobes. The upper surface is dark green, the lower surface is light green with some hairs in the nerves when young. They have attractive autumn tints. Yellowish-white, fragrant flowers are borne in small panicles. The fruits, 2.5cm (1in) long, are smooth, the wings nearly parallel. Very hardy. China and Manchuria, Korea and Japan. Introduced 1860.

'Durand's Dwarf' An attractive cultivar, growing to only 30–60cm (1–2ft). The leaves are small, 2.5–3.5cm (1–1½in) long, with bright red autumn colour.

'Flame' A selection with good autumn colour.

var. semenovii Leaves are smaller than the type and bright green. Afghanistan, Uzbekistan and Turkestan.

Acer giraldii

Pax (A. *caesium* subsp. *giraldii* (Pax) E. Murray)

A deciduous, open-crowned tree, to 15m (50ft) high, with brown or blackish-brown bark and roughish young branchlets covered in a glaucous bloom. The buds are large and brown. The thickish and rounded leaves are 10–12cm (4–5in) long with 3–5 lobes, the central one triangular, the lateral ones shorter, but all tapering at the tip and with wide sinuses. The base of the leaves is heart-shaped and their margins are coarsely and remotely toothed. The upper surface is smooth and blue-green, the lower surface is whitish-glaucous, with prominent veins and some hairs, especially when young. Greenish-yellow flowers are carried in terminal corymbs and are followed by brownish-yellow fruits, the nutlets convex and ridged, 3.5–5cm (1½–2in) long and spreading at acute angles. A rare maple. China. Introduced 1907.

Acer glabrum

Torr. Rock maple

A deciduous shrub or small tree, to 8m (25ft) high, with dark reddish-brown bark and long-pointed, bright red buds. The leaves are variable, but are usually 3-lobed, with short, taper-pointed tips and lightly heart-shaped bases. They are often deeply cut and coarsely toothed. The colour is dark glossy green above, paler beneath, and the stalks are reddish. The few flowers are greenish-yellow and carried in loose raceme-like corymbs on slender drooping stalks from the end of the branchlets. Smooth fruits, 2–2.5cm (¾–1in) long, are slightly spreading. An attractive maple with pretty autumn tints. Western USA. Introduced 1884.

subsp. douglasii (Hook.) Wesm. Branchlets purplish and leaves more deeply cut, 3-lobed, the lobes ovate, tapering and with wide, shallow sinuses.

Acer granatense

Boiss. (*A. opalus* subsp. *hispanicum* (Pourr.) E. Murray)

A deciduous, small tree or densely branched, large shrub, to 6m (20ft) high, with grey-brown bark and small, dark brown buds. The leaves are small with five blunt lobes. They are bright green above, lighter beneath with some hairs. Yellow flowers are borne in short, terminal umbels. Fruits are small and spread at a wide angle. Spain.

Acer grandidentatum

Torr. & A. Gray (*A. saccharum* subsp. *grandidentatum* (Torr. & A. Gray) Desmarais)

Big-toothed maple

A deciduous, small tree, to 10m (30ft) high, with brown, scaly bark and dark brown, pointed buds. The leaves are papery, 5–10cm (2–4in) across and 3–5-lobed. The lobes are acute or obtuse with broad, shallow sinuses and entire or slightly lobed margins. They are bright green above, slightly glaucous below with some hairs on the veins. Yellow flowers are borne on drooping stalks in short-stalked corymbs. They are followed by smooth fruits, 2.5cm (1in) long, spreading at about 60 degrees. An attractive maple, the leaves having beautiful autumn tints. Central to western USA. Introduced 1885.

Acer griseum

(Franch.) Pax Paper bark maple

A deciduous, medium-sized tree, to 12–15m (40–50ft) high. The bark is purplish or dark brown and scaly with thin, papery flakes. The buds are small and dark brown and the branchlets have some hairs at first. Papery leaves consist of three leaflets on a downy stalk. The leaflets are ovate-lanceolate, 5–6cm (2–2½in) long, and coarsely toothed. The flowers are yellow or greenish-yellow. They are carried in small cymes on pendent, downy stalks. The male and female flowers are separate (androdioecious); hermaphrodite flowers are never seen. Yellowish-brown fruits, with densely hairy nutlets, are 3–4cm (1¼–1½in) long and spreading at right angles. A very handsome maple on account of its peeling bark which hangs in large, loose flakes, revealing the lighter orange-coloured newer bark underneath. The leaves have attractive autumn tints. China. Introduced 1901.

Acer grosseri

Pax (*A. davidii* subsp. *grosseri* (Pax) P .C. de Jong)

A deciduous, small tree, to 11m (35ft) high, with purple or purplish-green branchlets that have white stripes later turning greyish-brown. The buds are small and dark brown. Papery, roundish-ovate leaves, 5–6cm (2–2½in) long, have 3–5 lobes, the central lobe being triangular and long taper-pointed, the lateral lobes being acute. The leaves are heart-shaped at the base with double-toothed margins. They are glossy dark green above; the lower surface is paler and covered with yellowish hairs when young, then hairless; there are prominent notches on the axil of the veins which help to identify the species. The leaves turn attractive tints in autumn. The flowers are greenish-yellow and are produced in slender, pendent racemes. Yellowish-brown fruits, 2–2.5cm (¾–1in) long, spread at right angles and almost horizontal. China. Introduced 1927.

var. hersii Found by Joseph Hers in 1919, has more distinctly lobed leaves and is said to have red bark striped with white. Some authors merge it with A. *grosseri*.

Acer heldreichii
Orph. ex Boiss.

A handsome, upright, deciduous, medium-sized tree, to 15m (50ft) high. This species has grey-brown bark, which is smooth or sometimes slightly fissured, and pointed, dark brown buds. The leaves, 10–15cm (4–6in) long, have 3–5 oblong-lanceolate lobes that are short and tapering at the tip with deep, narrow sinuses. They are coarsely toothed. The upper surface is dark green and smooth, except for some hairs at the base; the lower surface is paler with brown hairs along the principal vein. Yellow flowers are borne in short, broad corymbs, followed by smooth fruit, 3.5–5cm (1½–2in) long, that spread at about 60 degrees. Balkan States and Greece. Introduced 1879.

A botanist in Budapest informed me that two forms of this maple are found in the wild, one has leaves more deeply cut than the other.

Acer henryi
Pax

A deciduous, small tree, to 10m (30ft) high, with green, softly hairy branchlets that have a bluey bloom, later turning greeny-grey. The leaves are composed of three leaflets on a slender, reddish-brown common stalk. The leaflets, 6–10cm (2½–4in) long, are ovate, long and taper-pointed at the tip and wedge-shaped at the base. The margins are untoothed or lightly toothed. The upper surface of the leaves is bluey-green, the lower surface is paler but with some hairs on the veins. The flowers are yellowish and are borne in pendent racemes. Yellowish-brown fruits, 2–2.5cm (¾–1in) long, spread at right angles. This is a very handsome maple that is happy growing on all soils and has leaves with attractive tints in autumn. Male and female flowers appear on different trees (dioecious), and viable seed is not known: any fruits that may occur are not

A. *grosseri* var. *hersii* has leaves with distinct lobes and red bark with white stripes.

The popular and handsome A. *japonicum* 'Vitifolium' has deep green leaves that turn crimson and scarlet in autumn.

viable (parthenocarpic). China. Introduced 1903.

A maple labelled as A. *henryi* has been seen in Tashkent Botanic Gardens, Tashkent, Uzbekistan. I was told by Dr Belolipov, a botanist at the gardens, that it was grown from seed collected in China, so it is a first generation plant. It is quite different from A. *henryii* Pax: its branchlets are densely, softly hairy and the leaves are composed of three coarsely toothed leaflets, the central leaflet being broad-ovate, the two side leaflets being lanceolate. The leaves are similar to those of A. *negundo* but chemical analysis has shown it to be different from this species. Its true identity is yet to be ascertained.

Acer hookeri
Miq.

A deciduous, medium-sized tree, to 15m (50ft) high, with red branchlets that have some white markings, later turning greeny-grey. The buds are large, green and pointed. Thickish and wavy leaves are 10–18cm (4–7in) long and half as much wide. They are ovate and unlobed with finely toothed margins; the tip has a long, slender, tail-like point and the base is heart-shaped. The upper surface is bright glossy green and the lower surface is paler with prominent veins. The small flowers, on slender racemes, are greenish-yellow. They are followed by smooth fruit, 1–2cm (½–¾in) long, with curved wings spreading at angles of 90–120 degrees. This maple is tender. East Himalayas and south-west China. Cultivated since 1865.

Acer hyrcanum
Fisch. & C. A. Mey.

A deciduous, medium-sized tree, to 15m (50ft) high, with scaly, grey-brown bark and dark brown, short-pointed buds with several scales. The leaves are 5–10cm (2–4in) across and 5-lobed. The three central lobes are parallel-sided, each with several large, blunt teeth and narrow sinuses. The upper surface is bright green, while the lower surface is paler and rather glaucous; it is smooth except for a few hairs at the base along the chief vein. Greenish-yellow flowers are produced in corymbs on short stalks. They are followed by smooth fruits, 2–2.5cm (¾–1in) long and nearly parallel. A handsome maple, the leaves turning scarlet in autumn in its native land, but disappointing in Britain. South-east Europe and west Asia. Cultivated since 1865.

Acer japonicum
Thunb. ex Murray Full-moon maple

A deciduous, small tree, to 10m (30ft) high. The bark is smooth and greyish-brown and the buds are produced in pairs and have purple outer scales. They are rounded and densely, shaggily hairy. Roundish and 5–12cm (2–5in) long and wide, the leaves are shallowly 7–11-lobed. The lobes are broad-ovate and taper-pointed, with the margins sharply and irregularly toothed. The upper surface is deep green and smooth except for some hairs at the base; the lower surface is paler with whitish hairs where the blade joins the leaf stalk. Purplish-red flowers are produced in corymbs on long, drooping stalks. Yellowish-brown, smooth fruits are 2cm (¾in) long and spread at a wide angle, almost horizontally. A handsome maple, the leaves turning attractive tints of rich crimson in autumn. Japan. Introduced 1864.

'Aconitifolium' Leaves 7–9-lobed, the lobes deeply cut to the base, narrow at the bottom and then broadening. Margins sharply toothed and attractively cut. Rich autumn tints.

'Ezo-no-momiji' Leaves large and roundish with 11 shallowly cut and abruptly taper-pointed lobes. Attractive autumn tints.

'Green Cascade' Leaves roundish, 9–11-lobed, the base of each lobe narrow, being little wider than the mid-vein, then broadening out but deeply cut into narrow sections making a lace-like leaf. A handsome, low-growing pendent cultivar with beautiful autumn tints.

'Ô-isami' Leaves large, roundish, 10–12cm (4–5in) long and as much wide, 9–11-lobed, the lobes not deeply cut. Margins doubly toothed. A notable cultivar with attractive tints in autumn.

'Vitifolium' Leaves large, 10–12cm (4–5in) long and 12–18cm (5–7in) wide. There are 9–11 lobes, which are cut to the centre of the leaf, and have coarsely toothed margins. A handsome cultivar with rich tints of crimson and scarlet in autumn.

Acer kawakamii
Koid. (A. *caudatifolium*) Hayata

A deciduous, medium-sized tree, to 18m (60ft) high in the wild but smaller in cultivation. This species has green branchlets, later becoming greenish-grey with some white markings, and crimson, long-pointed buds. Papery leaves, 6–11cm (2½–4½in) long, are triangular, ovate to ovate-oblong without lobes and come to a long tail-like point at the tip. They are heart-shaped at the base with finely toothed margins. The upper surface is green and hairless; the lower surface is pale green with some hairs on the nerves at first then hairless. Purplish-white flowers are produced in racemes. Yellowish-brown fruit, 1–2cm (½–¾in) long, spread at obtuse angles. Taiwan. Introduced 1970.

Acer laevigatum
Wall.

An evergreen, small tree, to 10m (30ft) high, with green branchlets, later becoming yellowish-green or blackish-green. Small, pale pink buds are produced in pairs. The leaves are leathery, 12–18cm (5–7in) long, lanceolate or oblong-lanceolate without lobes and come to a long, tail-like point. They are heart-shaped at the base with margins that are saw-toothed when young, less so when mature. The upper surface is bright green and hairless; the lower surface is lighter and netted with veins (reticulate). The flowers are purplish-green and are borne in terminal corymbs, followed by brownish-yellow fruit, 3–4cm (1¼–1½in) long, which spread at acute angles. A tender tree. Himalayas, China. Introduced 1907.

Acer lanceolatum
Molliard

An evergreen, medium-sized tree, to 12m (40ft) or more, less in cultivation. The bark is greyish and the buds are small, light brown and pointed. Triangular, broad-ovate leaves are 6–9cm (2½–3½in) long, with a blunt tip. They are unlobed, with untoothed, wavy margins, and dark green above, glaucous below with attractively marked veins. Yellow flowers are carried in terminal corymbs. Small fruit, up to 1.5–2cm (½–¾in) long, spread at an angle of 80 degrees. A tender maple. Hong Kong. Introduced 1970.

Acer laxiflorum
Pax (A. *pectinatum* subsp. *laxiflorum* (Pax) E. Murray)

A deciduous, small tree, to 10m (30ft) high. Purple or greenish-purple branchlets have some white marks or stripes, later purplish-brown or dark brown. The buds

A. *japonicum* 'Aconitifolium' has deep green leaves with very deeply cut lobes and sharply toothed margins.

are brownish with some hairs. Papery deep green leaves, 5–10cm (2–4in) long, are 3- or rarely 5-lobed, the middle lobe longer than the side lobes. They are triangular and taper-pointed, with finely saw-toothed margins, and heart-shaped at the base. The lower surface is pale green with some reddish hairs on the nerves. Greenish-yellow flowers appear in pendent racemes, followed by brownish-yellow fruit, 2.5–4cm (1–1½in) long, spreading at obtuse angles. A handsome maple, but rare. China. Introduced 1908.

Acer leucoderme Small (*A. saccharum* subsp. *leucoderme* (Small) Desmarais) Chalkbark maple

A deciduous, medium-sized tree, to 15m (50ft) or more high, sometimes less in cultivation. The bark is light grey or greyish-brown; the buds are small, light brown, pointed and a little hairy. The leaves, 2.5–3.5cm (1–1½in) long, have 3–5 broad-ovate lobes, each terminating in a short, blunt point. They are heart-shaped or truncate at the base with wavy, toothed margins. The upper surface is yellowy-green; the lower surface is lighter and hairy. Yellow flowers are produced on slender pedicels. The fruits are hairy at first but smooth at maturity. They are 1.5–2cm (½–¾in) long and wide spreading. South-eastern USA. Introduced 1902.

Acer lobelii
Ten. (*A. cappadocicum* subsp. *lobelii* (Ten.) E. Murray)

An upright, deciduous tree, to 15m (50ft) or so high, with purplish branchlets that have a waxy bloom; they later become greyish. Greenish-purple and pointed buds. The papery, 10–18cm (4–7in) wide leaves are usually 5-lobed although young leaves are sometimes 3-lobed. The lobes are ovate, long taper-pointed, with wide and shallow sinuses and wavy, untoothed margins. The upper surface is dark green; the lower surface is paler with some tufts of hair. Yellow flowers are produced in corymbs that have short, upright stalks. Smooth fruits are 2.5–3.5cm (1–1½in) long and wide spreading. An attractive tree whose erect branches give it a columnar form. Italy. Introduced 1683.

Acer macrophyllum
Pursh Oregon maple

A deciduous, large tree, to 27m (90ft) or more, with dark grey and fissured bark; the buds are dark purple and obtuse. The leaves are large – 15–30cm (6–12in) across and 3–5-lobed. Each lobe is deeply cut, more than half way to the base of the leaf, and cut again into large, triangular minor lobes. The margins are untoothed or nearly so. They are dark shiny green above, covered with minute soft hairs when young; the lower surface is paler with tufts of white hairs in the axils of the veins. In autumn they turn golden-yellow. Fragrant, yellow flowers are produced in long racemes, followed by yellowish-brown fruits, the nutlets covered with long hairs. The fruits are 3.5–4.5cm (1½–1¾in) long and the wings spread at an angle of 60 degrees. A noble tree. Western North America. Introduced 1826.

'Kimballiae' Leaves deeply dissected, the lobes being cut almost to the base of the leaf. Very rare.

'Seattle Sentinel' This is an attractive form with an upright habit.

'Variegatum' Leaves green with white markings. Rare.

Acer mandshuricum
Maxim.

A deciduous, medium-sized tree, to 12m (40ft) high, with roughish, dark grey bark and dark brown, sharp-pointed buds with many scales. The leaves are papery and consist of three leaflets, 5–9cm (2–3½in) long, each on a long, slender stalk. The leaflets are oblong or oblong-lanceolate with long taper-pointed tips and saw-toothed margins. The upper surface is bright green and hairless; the lower surface is glaucous with hairs on the midrib. They turn an attractive purple in autumn. Yellowish-green corymbose flowers are often produced in threes. Yellowish-brown fruits have strongly convex nutlets; the wings, about 2.5–4.5cm (1–1¾in) long, spread at an acute angle. Manchuria, Korea and south-east Siberia. Introduced 1804.

Acer maximowiczii
Pax (*A. pectinatum* subsp. *maximowiczii* (Pax) E. Murray)

A deciduous, small tree, to 8m (25ft) high. This species has purple or reddish-purple branchlets, with some white markings, later becoming blackish-brown. The buds are smooth, reddish, acute and stalked. Triangular leaves, 5–7cm (2–3in) long, are 5-lobed, the middle lobe is elongated with a long, taper-pointed tip, the lateral lobes are ovate and the basal lobes are quite small.

The sinuses are taper-pointed and the margins are sharply toothed. The upper surface of the leaves is deep green and hairless; the lower surface is pale green with hairs on the axil of the veins. Yellowish-green flowers are produced in pendent racemes. Fruits are purple while young, brownish-yellow when mature; the nutlets are flat with wings, 2.5–3cm (1–1¼in) long, spreading at obtuse angles. An attractive maple. China. Introduced 1908.

Acer metcalfii

Rehder (A. *sikkimense* subsp. *metcalfii* (Rehder) P .C. de Jong)

A deciduous, small tree, to 10m (30ft) high, with purplish or yellowish-green branchlets, later blackish-yellow or dark brown. The coarsely saw-toothed leaves, 12–18cm (5–7in) long, have three triangular-ovate, taper-pointed lobes and heart-shaped or rounded bases. They are hairless, the upper surface is deep green, the lower surface paler. The flowers are yellowish-green and are produced in long racemes. They are followed by brownish-yellow fruits, 2–2.5cm (¾–1in) long and spreading at obtuse angles. A rare, tender and attractive maple. China. Introduced c1990.

Acer micranthum

Siebold & Zucc.

A deciduous, small tree, to 6m (20ft) high, with purplish branchlets that have distinct white markings, becoming greyish with age, and reddish-stalked buds. The bright green leaves are 5–6cm (2–2½in) long and wide and 5-lobed with narrow sinuses. Each lobe is ovate with a long, tail-like point. The margins are deeply and attractively cut. The underside is paler than the upper surface and is usually smooth but sometimes has a few hairs along the veins. Yellowish-green flowers are borne in long racemes. The nutlets with wings are 1cm (½in) long and spread at an obtuse angle. A very elegant maple with attractive autumn tints. Japan. Introduced 1879.

Acer miyabei

Maxim.

A deciduous, medium-sized tree, to 12m (40ft) high, with brown, corky bark and dark brown buds with 5–8 scales. The 5-lobed leaves are 10–15cm (4–6in) wide. The lobes are ovate with a long, blunt tip. Their margins are unevenly cut and wavy. Yellowish-green flowers are produced in corymbs. The fruits, which are covered with hairs, are 2–2.5cm (¾–1in) long and spread horizontally. A handsome, rare maple with yellow leaves in autumn. North Japan. Introduced 1892.

Acer mono

(A. *pictum*) Maxim.

A deciduous, large tree, up to 18m (60ft) high. The bark is grey and smooth, sometimes lightly fissured; the buds are reddish-brown and obtuse with many scales. The leaves are 10–18cm (4–7in) long with 5–7 ovate, taper-pointed lobes, the wide sinuses cut halfway to the base of the blade. The leaf bases are nearly heart-shaped and the margins are untoothed. The upper surface is deep green and smooth; the lower surface is pale green with some tufts of hair in the axils of the veins. Yellowish-green flowers are carried in terminal corymbs. They are followed by yellowish fruits with flat, compressed nutlets; the nutlets with wings

A. *miyabei* is a handsome maple with blunt-lobed leaves that are a stunning sight in autumn.

measure 2.5–3.5cm (1–1½in) long and spreading at obtuse angles or horizontally. An attractive maple, the leaves turning yellow in autumn. The leaves of this maple are variable in shape and there are many varieties. Japan, Manchuria, China. Introduced 1881.

'Hoshiyadori' A small tree, to 8m (25ft) high, with leaves that are speckled white and cream. An attractive cultivar.

'Shufu-nishiki' ('Akikaze-nishiki') Bark smooth. Leaves with white blotches. Some authors place this under A. *truncatum*, however, its smooth bark and matt leaves are more characteristic of A. *mono*.

var. mayrii (Schwer.) Nakai. Bark smooth. Leaves reddish when young, 5-lobed, the lobes short and broad, hairless. Flowers larger than the type, fruits often erect.

Acer monspessulanum

L. Montpelier maple

A deciduous, small tree, to 10m (30ft) or more, with a dense, rounded habit. The greyish bark is sometimes lightly fissured; the small buds are dark brown. Dark, glossy green leaves are leathery, 2.5–4cm (1–1½in) long and 3-lobed, with heart-shaped bases and untoothed margins. The lobes are triangular-ovate with blunt tips. The colour is paler beneath except for some down where the veins join the leaf stalk. Yellowish-green flowers are borne in corymbs on a long, slender stalk. The fruits are green or greenish-brown with wings 1–2cm (½–¾in) long and parallel. This is a neat and attractive maple and it sometimes turns yellow in autumn. South Europe, south-west Asia and North Africa. Introduced 1739.

subsp. cinerascens (Boiss.) Yalt. A small tree to 8m (25ft) high and usually multi-branched. The bark is dark grey, and the leaves, 2.5–6cm (1–2½in), are 3-lobed, the lobes triangular, coming to a blunt point, bright green above, paler beneath with some hairs. South-west Asia.

A. *morifolium* is an attractive large shrub or small tree, but may be a little tender.

subsp. turcomanicum (Pojark.) A. E. Murray A small, shrubby tree with 3-lobed, bright green leaves, paler beneath with some hairs. Caucasus.

Acer morifolium

Koidz. (*A. capillipes* subsp. *insulare* (Makino) A. E. Murray)

A deciduous, large shrub or small tree, to 8m (25ft) high, with green bark that has white markings. The ovate leaves are unlobed or remotely 3-lobed. They are hairless, bright green on the upper surface and pale green on the lower surface. The flowers are greenish-yellow and are carried in a short raceme. They are followed by small fruits, 1–2cm (½–¾in) long, spreading at an obtuse angle. An attractive maple, but may be a little tender. Southern Japan. Introduced c1994.

Acer morrisonense

Hayata (*A. rubescens* Hayata)

A deciduous, medium-sized tree, to 12m (40ft) or more, with purplish branches that have distinct white striations, and purplish buds. Papery, roundish-ovate leaves, 2.5–10cm (1–4in) long, are shallowly 5-lobed with more or less heart-shaped bases. The middle lobe is ovate and all the lobes have long, tapering tips and are forward-pointing with sharply toothed margins. They are bright glossy green above, pale green with hairs in the axils of the vein beneath. Racemes of yellowish-green flowers are followed by small, yellowish-brown fruits, 2–2.5cm (¾–1in) long and spreading at an angle of 90–110 degrees. A handsome maple with very attractive glossy foliage. Rare in cultivation. Taiwan. Introduced c1930.

'Millicent' A beautiful form, probably to about 3m (10ft) high. The foliage is pink when unfolding in spring, later dark green, mottled white and pink, then yellow and red in autumn. The branchlets are pink, later greeny-pink with white striations. A chance seedling, found in my nursery and named after my wife.

Bright glossy green leaves are a feature of the rare species *A. morrisonense*.

Acer negundo

L. Box elder

A deciduous, medium-sized tree, to 15m (50ft) or more, with greenish branchlets later becoming greeny-grey. The buds are acute and greenish-red; they leave conspicuous scars at the base of the branchlet, visible for two or three years. The leaves are divided into 3 or 5 leaflets and have long stalks. The leaflets are 5–10cm (2–4in) long, ovate, taper-pointed and have coarsely toothed margins. The upper side is bright green, while the underneath is paler and slightly hairy. Male and female flowers are carried on separate trees (dioecious). They are yellowish-green and do not have petals. The male flowers are produced in dense panicles, the females in slender, drooping racemes. The fruits are in long, slender racemes; the wings are 5–6cm (2–2½in) long and spread at an angle of six degrees. North America. Introduced 1688.

'Auratum' Branchlets green with a white bloom; leaflets wholly yellow, more green in the shade. Introduced 1891.

'Elegans' A small tree, growing slowly to 8m (25ft) high. Branchlets green with a bluey bloom. Leaves glossy green with a broad margin of yellow.

'Flamingo' A small tree or large shrub, to 8m (25ft) high. Branchlets greenish with a bluish bloom. The leaves are smaller than the type and usually have 5–7 white-margined, green leaflets. The young growth is red. Very attractive in spring.

'Kelly's Gold' A small tree, to 8m (25ft) high. Leaves bright clear yellow. A new cultivar from the USA.

A. *negundo* 'Flamingo' is a large shrub or small tree, grown for its eye-catching variegated foliage.

subsp. californicum (Torr. & A. Gray) Wesm. Young shoots and leaves downy but sometimes with a waxy, bluey bloom, the lower surface of the leaves covered with a grey down.

'Variegatum' A very old cultivar, the leaflets have an irregular border of white or are sometimes wholly white. The fruits are also variegated.

'Violaceum' A medium-sized tree, to 12m (40ft) high. Young branchlets are purplish and glaucous. The winter buds are larger than the type. The young leaves are purple-violet, later green. The flowers have purple-violet stamens and are very striking in spring as they open before the leaves.

Acer nigrum

Mich. (A. *saccharum* subsp. *nigrum* (Mich.) Desmarais) Black maple

A deciduous, medium-sized tree, to 15m (50ft) high, with deeply furrowed, dark brown to blackish bark and grey-brown, pointed and downy winter buds. The leaves are hairy when unfolding in spring. They are usually 5-lobed with broad sinuses. The lobes are broad-ovate and lobed, and the central lobe is sometimes almost parallel. The leaf bases are heart-shaped and the margins are untoothed. The upper surface is green with soft hairs; the lower surface is paler and densely covered with short, wool-like hairs. Yellow flowers are carried on long, hairy, bright red-brown stalks. The fruit is smooth, 2.5cm (1in) long and wide spreading. A handsome maple. Eastern USA. Introduced 1812.

Acer nikoense

Maxim. (A. *maximowiczianum* Miq.)
Nikko maple

A deciduous, medium-sized tree, to 14m (45ft) or more high. The buds are greyish-brown and hairy; the branchlets are greyish and densely hairy, becoming light grey. Each leaf has a stout, hairy stalk and is divided into three leaflets, 7–12cm (3–5in) long, the middle one is short stalked, the side ones are stalkless. The leaflets are ovate with long tapering tips and shallowly toothed margins. The upper surface is dark green; the lower surface is paler, almost glaucous; both surfaces are hairy. The yellow flowers, usually three together, are borne on drooping, hairy stalks. They are followed by dark brown fruits that have densely hairy nutlets, 3.5–5cm (1½–2in) long, spreading at an angle of up to 60 degrees. A handsome maple with attractive autumn tints of rich red or yellow. Japan, China. Introduced 1881.

Acer nipponicum

H. Hara

A deciduous, small tree, to 10m (30ft) or more, with rusty-brown, hairy branchlets, and greenish to reddish-purple and short-pointed buds. The leaves, 10–15cm (4–6in) long and 12–18cm (5–7in) across, are shallowly 5-lobed. The lobes are ovate and taper-pointed with coarsely toothed margins; the middle lobe is larger. The upper surface of the leaf is bright green, underneath is paler and softly hairy. Very long racemes of greenish flowers are produced, the males appearing first. The fruits are greenish, 2.5–3.5cm (1–1½in) long and wide-spreading. A very rare, handsome maple. Japan. Introduced c1930.

Acer oblongum

Wall. ex D.C.

An evergreen, small tree, to 10m (30ft) high, with grey or blackish-grey, fissured bark and small, brownish buds. Leathery leaves, 5–10cm (2–4in) long, are ovate-oblong, taper-pointed with untoothed margins. The upper surface is bright green and hairless; the lower surface is glaucous with the veins marked out. Flowers are yellow and produced in terminal panicles. They are followed by brownish-yellow fruits, 2.5–4cm (1–1½in) long, spreading at right angles. A tender maple. West China, Himalayas. Introduced 1824.

Acer obtusifolium

Sibth. & Sm. (*A. syriacum* Boiss. & Gaill.)

A large, semi-evergreen shrub or small tree, to 6m (20ft) high. The bark is light grey; the buds are dark brown. Hard and leathery leaves, 6–9cm (2½–3½in) long, are rhomboidal. When mature, they are usually unlobed, but they are shallowly 3-lobed when young. They do not lie flat but are concave and have heart-shaped bases with distinctly and sharply toothed margins. The colour is dark green on the upper surface, paler green on the lower surface and hairless. Greenish-yellow flowers are borne in lax terminal corymb-like cymes. The fruits are 2–2.5cm (¾–1in) long and spread at a wide angle. Eastern Mediterranean. Introduced c1903. *A. syriacum* so closely resembles this species to be almost indistinguishable.

Acer okamotoanum

Nakai (*A. mono* subsp. *okamotoanum* (Nakai) P. C. de Jong)

A deciduous, medium-sized tree, to 14m (45ft) or more high, with lightly fissured, reddish-brown branchlets, later brownish-grey or dark grey. The buds are greenish reddish-brown and rounded. Papery, deep green leaves, 7–14cm (3–5½in) long, are divided into seven triangular-ovate lobes, each coming to a sharp point. The margins are untoothed and slightly wavy. The lower surface is paler green, sometimes with some white hairs on the nerves. Greenish-yellow flowers are borne in terminal corymbs. The fruits are brownish, the nutlets flat. The wings are 5–6cm (2–2½in) long and spread at acute angles. This is an interesting maple, but quite rare, both in the wild and in cultivation. Only found on the island of Ullung-do. Introduced 1982.

Acer oliverianum

Pax

A deciduous, small tree, to 6m (20ft) high, with purplish-green, later greenish-brown branchlets, often with a waxy coating. The buds are small and greenish. Leaves are papery, with five ovate, taper-pointed, sharply saw-toothed lobes and truncate or nearly truncate bases. The sinuses reach halfway or more to the middle of the blade. The upper surface is dark yellowish-green; the lower surface is pale green with some white hairs. Purplish-green flowers, with white petals, are produced in terminal corymbs. They are followed by fruits that are purplish then brownish-yellow. The nutlets with wings, 2.5–3.5cm (1–1½in) long, spread nearly horizontally. An attractive maple with good autumn tints. China. Introduced 1901.

Acer opalus

Mill.

A deciduous, medium-sized tree of rounded habit and to 15m (50ft) or more high. This species has grey or dark grey bark, sometimes lightly fissured, and dark brown, ovoid, pointed winter buds with 10–12 scales. The leaves, 6–10cm (2½–4in) wide and somewhat less in length, have five shallow, broad-ovate lobes with short, taper-pointed tips and wide sinuses. They are heart-shaped at the base and have irregularly toothed margins. The upper surface is dark green, glossy and smooth; the under surface is paler and downy, especially along the main veins. The flowers are yellow and borne in crowded short-stalked corymbs. Brownish fruits follow and have nutlets to 3.5cm (1½in) long, varying considerably in divergence. A handsome maple, particularly attractive in spring with its yellow flowers. North Africa. Introduced 1752.

subsp. obtusatum (Willd.) Gams Has larger, thicker leaves, to 14cm (5½in) wide, with more rounded lobes. The leaf underside is densely woolly and the flower stalks are hairy. In the wild, the leaves turn yellow in autumn, but this is not marked in cultivation.

Acer palmatum

Thunb. ex Murray Japanese maple

A deciduous, medium-sized tree of rounded shape, to 12m (40ft) or more. The branchlets are green or purplish-green becoming blackish-grey and the buds are smallish and always in pairs. Papery, rounded leaves,

The well-known Japanese maple, *A. palmatum*, has given rise to many beautiful and popular cultivars.

5–9cm (2–3½in) long, have 5–7 ovate, oblong-lanceolate lobes. They are taper-pointed or long, taper-pointed, with acute sinuses reaching half or one-third of the way to the middle of the blade, and heart-shaped at the base. The margins are doubly toothed. The upper surface is deep green and hairless, while the lower surface is pale green with tufts of white hairs at the axil of the veins. Small flowers are carried in corymbs on long, purple stalks. Smooth fruits are brownish-yellow, with wings 1–2.5cm (½–1in) long, spreading at an obtuse angle. This handsome species produces a fiery autumn colour. It has many attractive cultivars. These are featured separately, see pp.91–115. Japan, China, Korea. Introduced 1820.

subsp. amoenum (Carrière) H. Hara Leaves larger, 7–12cm (3–5in) wide, palmately 7–9-lobed. The lobes are broad-ovate, abruptly taper-pointed with taper-pointed sinuses reaching to the middle of the blade. Margins finely toothed. Japan, China, Korea.

subsp. matsumurae Koidz. Leaves 5–7cm (2–3in) wide, usually 5-lobed with two small basal lobes. The lobes are ovate-lanceolate, taper-pointed with narrow sinuses reaching to the base of the leaf. Margins saw-toothed. Japan.

Acer paxii
Franch.

An evergreen, small tree, to 10m (30ft) high, with green branchlets, later ash-grey to brown, and brownish winter buds. Smooth, leathery leaves, 7–12cm (3–5in) long, are entire or occasionally 3-lobed, the middle lobe short, taper-pointed, the lateral lobes shorter. The margins are wavy with some teeth. The upper surface is deep shiny green, while the lower surface is glaucous. Flowers are borne in terminal corymbs and are whitish-yellow. They are followed by greenish-brown fruits with convex nutlets. The wings, including the nutlets, are 2.5–3cm (1–1¼in) long and spread at an obtuse angle. A tender maple growing well in the south of France and in other warmer climates. South-west China.

Acer pectinatum
Wall. ex G. Nicholson

A deciduous, small tree, to 10m (30ft) or more, with purple branchlets that have some white striations, later brown, and reddish winter buds. Papery leaves, 7–15cm (3–6in) long, are usually 3-lobed but sometimes have two additional small basal lobes; they are heart-shaped at the base. The lobes are ovate with sharply tapering points and have sharply saw-toothed margins with a red line marked out on the edge of the leaf. The upper surface is bright green; the lower surface is paler with some reddish hairs, especially when young. Yellow flowers are borne in racemes and are followed by fruits on short stalks. Wings with nutlets are 2.5cm (1in) long and spread almost horizontally. An attractive maple and interesting as the only snake bark from the Himalayas. East Himalayas and south-west China.

Acer pensylvanicum
L. Moose wood maple

A deciduous, small tree, to 8m (25ft) high, often shrubby in the wild. The green bark is attractively striped with white lines, later reddish-brown, and the winter buds are red and 2-scaled. Large leaves, 12–18cm (5–7in) long and with heart-shaped bases, are 3-lobed; the middle lobe is broad-ovate and all lobes are forward-pointing with long, taper-pointed tips and finely and sharply double-toothed margins. The upper surface is bright green; the lower surface is paler with reddish hairs, especially when young. Yellow flowers are borne in pendent racemes, followed by yellowish-brown fruits. Wings with nutlets are 2cm (¾in) long, convex and wide-spreading. A handsome maple, the leaves turning butter-yellow in autumn, preferring a soil not too alkaline. Eastern North America. Introduced 1755.

'Erythrocladum' Young shoots are a brilliant bright crimson, later with yellowish lenticels. Leaves are smaller, 3-lobed, the two side lobes not so forward-pointing. This attractive maple hates lime soil and may be difficult to establish. Introduced 1904.

Acer pentaphyllum
Diels

A deciduous, small tree, to 10m (30ft) or more, with brownish-yellow branchlets, later light brown, deeply fissured and roughish. The buds are dark brown-blackish, pointed and have several scales. Deep green leaves are usually divided into five finger-like lobes, which are very narrow at the base, as if on a short stalk, and have tapering tips. The lower surface is whitish-glaucous. The leaves have long stalks – 10–11cm (4–4½in). Yellowish flowers are borne in corymbs. Brownish-yellow fruits have wings with nutlets that are 2.5–3cm (1–1¼in) long. A very distinct species, this is one of the most handsome and rare of maples, but tender. China. Introduced c1930.

Acer pilosum
Maxim.

A deciduous, small tree, to 10m (30ft) high, with yellowish-grey branchlets, later brownish-grey, and dark brown buds. The leathery leaves, 4–5cm (1½–2in) long, have three oblong-ovate lobes, the lateral ones wide-spreading. They are nearly heart-shaped at the base, and the margins are nearly untoothed or rarely have a few teeth. The upper surface is deep green and smooth or slightly softly hairy; the lower surface is pale green, with a network of veins and with hairs on the nerves. Small, yellowish-green flowers are borne in short racemes, male and female in separate clusters. Small, downy fruits have wings with nuts 3.5–5cm (1½–2in) long and parallel. An interesting maple, recently introduced. China. Introduced c1997.

The tender species *A. paxii* has smooth, leathery, evergreen leaves that are unlobed or may have three lobes.

Acer platanoides
L. Norway maple

A deciduous, large tree, to 27.5m (90ft) high, with grey or grey-black lightly fissured bark and green or, in some cultivars, purple winter buds. The 5-lobed leaves are 10–18cm (4–7in) wide and almost as long, with heart-shaped bases. The three middle lobes are parallel sided and forward pointing; the two basal ones spread outwards. They are all taper-pointed, remotely toothed and bright shiny green on both surfaces; the undersides are smooth, except for some tufts of hair in the axil of the veins. The long stalks exude milky sap when broken. Greenish-yellow flowers are produced in mid-spring, just before the leaves, in erect branching corymbs. Fruits are carried on long stalks; wings with nutlets are 3.5–5cm (1½–2in) long and wide-spreading. Europe. Introduced 1604.

'Cleveland' An upright tree with red-toned young leaves, later bright green. One of several selections that have been made in the United States, which include the upright **'Omstead'** and **'Crimson Sentry'** (see below).

'Columnare' A medium-sized, upright tree, reaching 18m (60ft).

'Crimson King' Buds dark purple; leaves deep crimson-purple throughout the summer.

'Crimson Sentry' A small tree, to 8m (25ft) high, multi-branched; leaves deep red to purple, fastigiate and slow growing.

PLATE IV

Acer palmatum and *cultivars*

A. *palmatum* 'Shishigashira'

A. *palmatum* 'Shindesmojo'

A. *palmatum* 'Ôsakazuki'

A. *palmatum*
'Bloodgood'

A. *palmatum* 'Butterfly'

All leaves are shown at approximately half lifesize

A. *palmatum* 'Karasugawa'

A. *palmatum* 'Ighigyoji'

A. *palmatum* subsp. *matsumurae*

A. *palmatum* 'Shaina'

A. *palmatum* 'Okushimo'

A. *platanoides* 'Nanum' is a small tree with leaves that are smaller than the species.

'Cucullatum' Leaves long-stalked and fan-shaped, with truncate bases that have seven or nine prominent veins instead of the usual five.

'Dissectum' Leaves 3-lobed, cut to the leaf base, the basal pair often cut almost as deeply again, all lobes divided into secondary lobes with drawn-out points.

'Drummondii' Leaves broadly edged with white.

'Globosum' A small tree, to 10m (30ft) high, with a dense, round shape.

'Goldsworth Purple' Leaves light reddish-brown and wrinkled when young.

'Laciniatum' (Eagle's claw maple) A smaller tree, more erect in habit. Leaves with lobes ending in long, often curved, claw-like points, often truncate at base.

'Nanum' ('Pyramidale') A slow-growing tree, 5–6m (15–20ft) high, with smaller leaves and short internodes.

'Palmatifidum' Similar to 'Dissectum' (above). Leaves on long stalks, 5–7-lobed, lobes often overlapping each other; each lobe is fan-shaped, divided into secondary lobes, taper-pointed.

'Reitenbachii' Leaves reddish when young, later reddish-green, then dark red in autumn.

'Schwedleri' Leaves bright red when young, later becoming green. An attractive cultivar, the yellow flowers contrasting nicely with the young reddish-purple leaves.

Acer pseudoplatanus
L. Sycamore

A deciduous, large tree, to 30m (100ft) or more high, with greyish-brown bark, attractively peeling off in large flakes. Winter buds are large, rounded and greenish. The leaves, 10–18cm (4–7in) across, are 5-lobed with heart-shaped bases. The lobes are ovate, taper-pointed with coarsely toothed margins. They are dark green and hairless above, paler and dull glaucous on the lower surface with some pale brown hairs in the axil of the veins. Yellowish flowers appear in long racemes. Fruits are on long pendent racemes; wings with nutlets are 3–5cm (1¼–2in) long, spreading at an angle of about 60 degrees. South and central Europe. Introduced fourteenth century.

'Atropurpureum' Leaves dark green above, rich purple beneath.

'Brilliantissimum' Leaves are a beautiful pinkish shade when unfolding, dull green on the underside. A handsome variety, but slow growing. (See also 'Prinz Handjéry'.)

'Corstorphinense' Leaves pale yellow when young, golden in early summer.

'Erythrocarpum' Fruits red, borne on pink stalks.

'Leopoldii' Leaves attractively marked with white blotches, sometimes also pinkish when unfolding in spring, dull green on the under side. (See also A. *pseudoplatanus* 'Nizetii'.)

'Nizetii' Resembles 'Leopoldii', but the underside of the leaf is purple.

'Prinz Handjéry' This maple resembles 'Brilliantissimum'. The leaves are striking salmon-pink in spring but the underside is purple.

'Simon-Louis Frères' A small tree, to about 10m (30ft) high. The leaves have cream and pink margins; the pink is especially noticeable when young.

'Worley' Leaves rich yellow; stalks reddish.

Acer pseudosieboldianum
(Pax) Kom.

A deciduous, small tree, to 8m (25ft) high, with greenish or greenish-purple branchlets, later grey or greyish-brown. The large, reddish buds have six scales and are softly hairy. Rounded leaves are papery, 7–9cm (3–3½in) in diameter and heart-shaped at the base. They are usually 9–11-lobed, the lobes triangular-ovate, taper-pointed and with double-toothed margins. The sinuses are taper-pointed and are cut halfway to the middle of the blade. The upper surface is deep green and hairless; the lower surface is light green with white hairs on the nerves. Flowers are reddish with white petals and are carried in corymbs. The yellowish fruits have convex nutlets and wings 2.5–3cm (1–1¼in) long and wide-spreading. A handsome maple, with leaves turning attractive tints of crimson in the autumn. North-east China, Korea.

Acer pubipalmatum
W. P. Fang

A deciduous, small tree, to 10m (30ft) high, with densely white-hairy, green or purplish-green branchlets, later grey or blackish-grey and lightly fissured, and purple buds. The 5-lobed leaves have saw-toothed margins and are 3.5–5cm (1½–2in) long and a little wider. The lobes are lanceolate and taper-pointed, truncate at the base. The sinuses are acute, reaching to four-fifths of the way to the middle of the blade. The upper surface of the leaves is deep green, hairy when young; the lower surface is pale green with densely hairy primary veins. The leaf stalks are hairy when young. Andromonoecious flowers are purple and produced in corymbs. They are followed by purplish-brown, roundish fruits;

Sycamore, *A. pseudoplatanus*, has many interesting cultivars. This one, 'Leopoldii', has white-mottled leaves.

the wings with nutlets are 2cm (¾in) long and spread at an obtuse angle. An attractive maple, rare and little known. China.

Acer pycnanthum
K. Koch

A deciduous, medium-sized tree, to 12m (40ft) or more. The branchlets are reddish-purple, later greyish and roughish; the large buds are reddish. Papery leaves, 7cm (3in) long, are shallowly 3-lobed, the central lobe broad-ovate and taper-pointed. The margins are irregularly toothed. The leaves are deep bronze-purple when unfolding in spring, maturing deep green above, glaucous below. Reddish flowers appear in early spring. Smooth, erect fruits, 2cm (¾in) long, ripen in early summer. A handsome maple, rare in cultivation, with beautiful autumn tints, preferring a neutral to acid soil. Japan. Introduced c1978 (see also p.125).

Acer robustum
Pax

A deciduous, small tree, to 8m (25ft) high, with purplish-brown branchlets, later olive-brown, and purplish-red buds. The leaves are papery, 6–7cm (2½–3in) long and 7–9-lobed. The lobes are ovate and taper-pointed with sinuses reaching nearly to the middle of the blade. They are truncate at the base and have irregularly saw-toothed margins. The leaves are slightly hairy on both surfaces when young, then smooth above, with tufts of hair on the nerves below. Reddish flowers with greenish-white petals are produced in corymbs. Greenish-yellow fruits are 2.5–4cm (1–1½in) long and spread horizontally. A handsome maple, differing from *A. palmatum* chiefly in its larger fruits, recently introduced (about 1998) and still rare. China.

Acer rubrum
L. Red maple

A deciduous, large tree, to 30m (100ft) in the wild, with reddish branchlets later greyish and scaly. The buds are reddish and obtuse. Papery leaves, 7–10cm (3–4in) long, are 3–5-lobed with rounded bases. The lobes are triangular with short, tapering tips, the central lobe being the longest. They are dark lustrous green above and glaucous beneath with some hairs, especially along the veins. Rich red flowers on reddish stalks, appear in dense clusters before the leaves in early spring. The fruits, on long, slender, pendent stalks, ripen in early summer; the wings with nutlets are 2cm (¾in) long, spreading at an angle of 60 degrees. A handsome maple with rich autumn tints. North America. Introduced 1835.

Rich and varied autumn colours are a feature of the rare and handsome *A. pycnanthum*.

'Bowhall' An upright maple, to 11–12m (35–40ft).

'Columnare' An upright tree, to 15m (50ft) high, narrower than 'Bowhall' but not as narrow as 'Scanlon'.

'October Glory' An upright tree with relatively thick, dark green leaves. Brilliant autumn colours.

'Red Sunset' A fine tree with a broad pyramidal crown. Leaves turn an attractive colour in autumn.

'Scanlon' A narrow, columnar tree. Leaves turning attractive tints of orange or red.

'Schlesingeri' An old cultivar. Leaves turning rich orange-yellow to red in autumn.

var. trilobum Torr. & A. Gray ex K. Koch A smaller tree with smaller, 3-lobed leaves that are rounded and are usually hairy underneath. Rich autumn tints.

In the United States, many other cultivars have been selected for their autumn colour, including **'Autumn Spire'** and **'Burgundy Belle'**.

Acer rufinerve

Siebold & Zucc.

A deciduous, medium-sized, upright tree, to 12m (40ft) high, with green branchlets that have a waxy bloom, later becoming green with jagged white stripes. The buds are also green with a waxy bloom and have stalks. Leaves, 6–12cm (2½–5in) long, are 3-lobed sometimes with two small basal lobes, and are heart-shaped at the base. The middle lobe is triangular, the lateral lobes almost at right angles and shorter. They have irregularly toothed margins. The upper surface is dark green and smooth; the lower surface is paler with reddish down along the veins. Greenish-yellow flowers in erect racemes are followed by yellowish-green or yellowish-brown fruits; the nutlets with wings are 1–2cm (½–¾in) long, spreading at obtuse or right angles. Rich autumn tints; upright in habit. Japan. Introduced 1879.

'Albolimbatum' A small tree, up to 10m (30ft) high, with irregularly white-marked green leaves. This plant can be very variable in its leaf markings if propagated by seed. Very attractive.

Acer saccharinum

L. Silver maple

A deciduous, large tree, to over 30m (100ft) high, with light grey, fissured and shaggy bark and reddish buds. The leaves are 10–15cm (4–6in) long and 5-lobed with heart-shaped bases. The lobes are ovate-lanceolate and taper-pointed with deep, wide sinuses cut to two-thirds of the way to the middle of the blade. The margins are irregularly toothed. The upper surface is light green, the lower surface lighter and glaucous. Petal-less, greenish-yellow flowers appear in early spring. The fruits, 3.5–5cm (1½–2in) long, on slender, pendent stalks, ripen in early summer; the wings are round-ended and spread at an obtuse angle. A handsome maple, the leaves showing their silvery undersides in the wind. Eastern North America. Introduced 1725.

'Born's Gracious' An elegant tree of slightly weeping habit. Leaves deeply cut, almost to the base of the blade, the segments narrow and deeply toothed.

'Laciniatum Wieri' This maple has more deeply dissected leaves with narrow and more sharply toothed lobes. The branches are pendent.

'Lutescens' Leaves are orange-yellow when young, later yellowish.

'Pyramidale' A columnar tree.

Acer saccharum

Marshall Sugar maple

A deciduous, large tree, to over 30m (100ft) in the

wild, a little less in cultivation. It has dark grey, fissured and scaly bark, and dark brown, acute winter buds. The smooth, papery leaves are 7–12cm (3–5in) across with heart-shaped bases. They have 3–5 abruptly tapering and untoothed lobes, the central lobe parallel with wide notches. The sinuses are deeply cut, to about two-thirds of the way to the middle of the leaf blade. The upper surface is deep yellowish-green; the lower surface is paler, and shows silvery in the wind. The slender stalks exude no milky sap when broken. Flowers are produced in clusters and are petal-less and greenish-yellow. The smooth, brownish fruits have nutlets with wings 2–3.5cm (¾–1½in) long and almost parallel. A handsome maple with rich autumn colour, growing in all soils. Eastern North America. Introduced 1735.

'Brocade' A small tree with 3–5-lobed leaves. The sinuses are cut almost to the base of the leaf. The lobes are ovate and triangular – narrow at base and broadening at the tip; each lobe is subdivided into two or three smaller, long-tapering lobes.

'Newton Sentry' A fastigiate tree, to 12m (40ft) high. This cultivar resembles 'Temple's Upright' (below) but lacks a single central leader. It has vertical branches, the lateral ones short and stubby.

subsp. floridanum (Chapm.) Desmarais A small tree to 10m (30ft) high. Leaves roundish with heart-shaped bases and 3–5 lobes; the lobes short, obtuse. They are bright green on the upper surface with a few hairs when unfolding in spring; the lower surface is paler with some hairs. Several cultivars have been selected in the United States for their autumn colour, including **'Commemoration'** and **'Majesty'**.

subsp. skutchii (Rehder) A. E. Murray. A medium-sized tree, to 15m (50ft) high in the wild. The branchlets are purple. Leaves, 12–15cm (5–6in) long, are 5-lobed. They are brilliant crimson-pink when unfolding in the spring. Attractive tints in autumn. Mexico, Guatemala. Introduced 1992.

'Temple's Upright' Columnar with a strong-growing central leader. Handsome; good autumn colour.

Acer sempervirens

L.

A deciduous or semi-evergreen, large shrub or small tree, to 8m (25ft) high. The bark is greyish-brown; the buds are dark brown. Leathery leaves of various shapes are 2.5–5cm (1–2in) long, bright green and smooth on both surfaces. They are sometimes ovate and sometimes 3-lobed, the lobes rounded and blunt, usually obtuse at the base and with untoothed margins. The flowers are yellowish and are carried in corymbs. Fruits, sometimes with a reddish tinge on the wings, are smooth; the nutlets and wings, 1–2cm (½–¾in) long, are parallel or spread at an angle of 60 degrees. Eastern Mediterranean. Introduced 1752.

Acer serrulatum

Koidz. (*A. oliverianum* subsp. *formosanum* (Koidz.) A. E. Murray)

A deciduous, large tree, to 23m (70ft) in the wild, but smaller in cultivation. The branchlets are green and the bark is greeny-grey. The winter buds are green with a touch of redness. Papery leaves, 7–9cm (3–3½in) long and 7–11cm (3–4½in) wide, are palmately 5-lobed. The lobes are triangular and ovate, the middle lobe a little longer than the side lobes. They are long-tapering with wide sinuses and irregularly toothed margins. The upper surface is bright green, the lower surface pale green and finely netted. Yellow flowers are borne in terminal cyme-like inflorescences. Fruits are yellowish-brown; nutlets with wings are 2.5cm (1in) long and spread at 90–120 degrees. A graceful maple but not suitable for colder gardens. Taiwan. Introduced 1980.

Acer shirasawanum

Koidz.

A deciduous, small tree, to 10m (30ft) high, with greyish-brown bark, often lightly marked with grey-green lines. The winter buds are ovoid and acute. Papery, roundish leaves, 9–11cm (3½–4½in) across, are palmate. There are eleven ovate, taper-pointed lobes with wide sinuses, cut to about one-third of the way to the middle of the blade, and sharply toothed margins. They are bright green above, paler underneath with some white hairs in the vein axils. Pale yellow flowers appear in upright corymbs (a feature that has led to the selections 'Aureum' and 'Microphyllum', below, being moved here from *A. japonicum*). They are followed by smooth, greenish-brown fruits, about 2cm (¾in) long and horizontally spreading. The leaves turn yellow and scarlet in the autumn. Japan. Introduced 1907.

'Aureum' (*A. japonicum* 'Aureum') Leaves bright yellow in spring, yellow in summer, yellow-orange to red in autumn. Slow-growing but very decorative.

A. *shirasawanum* 'Aureum' has yellow leaves that turn from yellow-orange to red in autumn.

'Microphyllum' (A. *japonicum* 'Microphyllum') A large shrub or small tree, to 5m (15ft) high. Leaves smaller than the type, usually 11-lobed, sometimes 9-lobed. Attractive tints in autumn.

var. tenuifolium Koidz. (A. *tenuifolium* (Koidz) Koidz) A large shrub or small tree, to 8m (25ft) high. Branchlets green; winter buds purplish-red, ovoid. Leaves papery, roundish and 5–7cm (2–3in) wide; the lobes are ovate and long-tapering with acute sinuses that are sometimes cut to the middle of the blade. The leaves are heart-shaped at the base; the upper surface is bright green and smooth except for some hairs on young leaves; the underneath is paler with hairs in the axil of the veins. The flowers are yellow with a red-purple hue and are carried in corymbs. Fruits are lightly hairy or smooth; the wings are ascending – nutlets with wings about 2cm (¾in) wide. A graceful maple with good autumn tints. Japan.

Acer sieboldianum

Miq.

A deciduous, large shrub or small tree, to 6m (20ft) high, with reddish-brown or purplish, softly hairy branches, and ovate, smooth winter buds, the terminal bud lacking. The leaves are roundish, papery, 6–9cm (2½–3½in) across, shallowly heart-shaped at the base and with 7–9 ovate, long-tapering lobes. The margins are sharply saw-toothed. The upper leaf surface is bright green, the lower surface is paler, with some hairs on the vein axils. Small, pale yellow flowers are carried in corymbs. They are followed by smooth, greenish-brown fruits; the nutlets with wings are 1–2cm (½–¾in) long and spread horizontally. Japan. In cultivation 1880.

'Sode-no-uchi' A dwarf shrub to 1.8–2.2m (6–7ft) high, slow growing. Leaves usually 11-lobed.

Acer sinense

Pax (A. *campbellii* subsp. *sinense* (Pax) P. C. de Jong)

A deciduous, small tree, to 5m (15ft) high. The branchlets are greenish at first, later yellowish-brown or dark brown and smooth. The small winter buds have six scales covered by the base of the stalk. Leaves, 10–15cm (4–6in) long, are palmately 5-lobed and have heart-shaped bases. The lobes are ovate and taper-pointed with acute sinuses reaching more or less

halfway to the middle of the blade. They have saw-toothed margins. The upper surface is deep green and smooth; the lower surface is pale green with some tufts of yellowish hairs on the vein axils. Greenish-white flowers are borne in terminal panicles. Yellowish, usually smooth fruits have nutlets with wings 3.5cm (1½in) long, spreading at acute angles or horizontally. A handsome maple, preferring warmer gardens. China. Introduced 1901.

Acer sinopurpurascens
W. C. Cheng

A deciduous, small tree, to 10m (30ft) high, with smooth, grey bark and branchlets that are slightly hairy when young. The winter buds are brown and ovoid, with numerous scales. The leaves are papery in texture and have 3–5 lobes with untoothed or remotely toothed margins. The middle three lobes are parallel, oblong and taper-pointed. They are deep green above, pale green below; both surfaces are hairy when young, then slightly hairy, with tufts of hair at the axil of the nerve. The stalks are slender. Reddish-purple flowers are produced in corymb-like racemes, followed by brownish-yellow fruits with hairy wings; wings with nutlets are 2.5–3cm (1–1¼in) long and spreading nearly erectly. A very rare maple. China. In cultivation 1980.

Acer spicatum
Lam. Mountain maple

A deciduous, large shrub or a small tree, to 8m (25ft) high and often multi-trunked. The branchlets are reddish-purple and covered with soft down, later becoming greyish-brown and smooth. The winter buds are acute and have densely woolly, bright red outer scales. The leaves, 7–12cm (3–5in) long, have 3–5 broad-ovate and long-tapering lobes with acute sinuses cut one-third of the way to middle of the blade. The leaf margins are coarsely toothed and the bases are heart-shaped. The upper surface is yellowish-green; the underside is paler; both sides are hairy when unfolding in spring, and later the upper surface is smooth, but the lower surface is densely woolly. The stalks are slender and reddish. Yellowish flowers are produced in upright compound racemes. Reddish-brown fruits have nutlets with wings about 1cm (½in) long, spreading at an angle of 90 degrees. A handsome maple with leaves turning attractive tints of red or yellow in autumn. Eastern USA, Canada. Introduced 1750.

A. *sieboldianum* is a large shrub or small tree with something of interest all year round.

Acer taronense
Hand.-Mazz. (A. *pectinatum* subsp. *taronense* (Hand.-Mazz.) A. E. Murray)

A small, spreading, deciduous tree, to 10m (30ft) high. Reddish-purple branchlets sometimes have some white marks, later blackish-brown. The winter buds are reddish, the scales slightly hairy on their margins. Papery leaves, 6–15cm (2½–6in) long and with heart-shaped bases, have five ovate, long-tapering lobes with sharply saw-toothed margins; the middle lobe is longer than the side lobes. The sinuses are acute and cut one-third of the way to the middle of the leaf blade. The upper surface is deep green and smooth; the lower surface is pale green with reddish hairs and conspicuous veins especially when young. Dioecious, yellowish-green flowers appear on simple racemes, followed by purplish-yellow fruit, the nutlets flat. Wings with nutlets are 2–2.5cm (¾–1in) long, spreading at an obtuse angle. A handsome maple with attractive foliage. China, north Burma. Introduced 1924.

Acer tataricum
L.

A deciduous, large shrub or small tree, to 10m (30ft) high, with light grey, smooth bark and small, brownish buds. The leaves are round, 5–9cm (2–3½in) long and unlobed or lightly 3-lobed with heart-shaped bases; the central lobe is broad-ovate and short-tapering. The margins are irregularly toothed. The upper surface is bright green and smooth and the lower surface is paler with some down. Flowers are greenish-white and carried in erect panicles. Brown or reddish-brown fruits have nutlets with wings 2–2.5cm (¾–1in) long, almost parallel. A pretty maple, especially in spring when the leaves are reddish-purple. East Europe, Turkey, Caucasus. Introduced 1759.

Acer tegmentosum
Maxim.

A deciduous, medium-sized tree, to 12m (40ft) high, producing green branchlets with white striations and a white, waxy bloom, later grey with white markings. The buds are red with hairy scales. Papery leaves, 6–15cm (2½–6in) long, less across, are usually 3-lobed but sometimes shallowly 5-lobed. They are heart-shaped at the base with sharply saw-toothed margins. The lobes are ovate with tapering tips and forward-pointing with wide but deeply cut sinuses. The upper surface is deep green and smooth, while the lower surface is pale green with some yellowish hairs at the axil of the veins. Bears slender, pendent racemes of yellowish-green flowers, followed by smooth, yellowish-brown fruits; nutlets with wings, 2.5–4cm (1–1½in) long, spread at a wide angle. A beautiful maple, the leaves with tints of yellow in the autumn. China, Manchuria, Korea, east Siberia. Cultivated c1880.

Acer tenellum
Pax

A deciduous, small tree, to 8m (25ft) high, with purplish branchlets, later grey and smooth, and ovoid, greenish winter buds. The papery leaves are 5–7cm (2–3in) long and heart-shaped at the base. They are usually 3-lobed, the middle lobe obtuse and acute. The upper surface is deep green and smooth, the lower pale green with some hairs in the vein axils. Yellowish-green flowers are produced in terminal corymbs. Smooth, brown fruits have nutlets with wings 2–2.5cm (¾–1in) long and spreading nearly horizontally. An attractive maple, sometimes grown incorrectly as A. *mono* var. *tricuspis*. China. Introduced 1901.

Acer tetramerum
Pax

A deciduous, small tree, to 6–8m (20–25ft) high, with purple branchlets, later greyish- or blackish-brown and ovoid, purplish winter buds. The leaves are papery and 5–9cm (2–3½in) long. They are ovate, unlobed or shallowly 3-lobed, long-tapering, rounded at the base and have coarsely toothed margins. The upper surface is deep green; the lower surface is lighter green with tufts of white hairs on the axil of the veins. Dioecious,

A. *triflorum* has papery, dark green leaves that are divided into three long leaflets.

greenish-yellow flowers are borne in slender racemes, followed by yellowish-brown fruits with wrinkled nutlets and with the wings 5–6cm (2–2½in) long, spreading at an angle of about 60 degrees. An elegant maple with the leaves turning red in autumn. China. Introduced 1901.

Acer thomsonii

Miq. (*A. sterculiaceum* subsp. *thomsonii* (Miq.) E. Murray)

A deciduous, medium-sized tree, to 14m (45ft) or more high, with greyish-brown bark and dark brown buds with several scales. The large leaves, up to 30cm (12in) or more long and as much wide, are produced on long stalks and have heart-shaped bases. They are 3-lobed, the central lobe triangular and larger than the side lobes. The sinuses are wide and the margins are untoothed and wavy. Yellowish-green flowers are produced in racemes. Brown fruits are 5–7cm (2–3in) long. An interesting but tender maple, very rare. Himalayas. Introduced 1835.

Acer trautvetteri

Medw. (*A. heldreichii* subsp. *trautvetteri* Medw.) (E. Murray)

A medium-sized, deciduous tree, to 15m (50ft) or more high, with dark red-purplish branchlets that later become grey-brown, fissured and scaly. The winter buds are dark brown. The leaves are 7–18cm (3–7in) long with five ovate lobes, heart-shaped bases and coarsely toothed margins. The sinuses are acute, sometimes cut almost to the base of the leaf but sometimes less so. The leaves are dark lustrous green, paler beneath, where there are tufts of down in the vein axils. The stalks are slender and red. Yellow flowers are borne in erect corymbs, followed by smooth, red fruits, the wings sometimes keeled. Nutlets with wings are 4.5–5cm (1¾–2in) long and parallel. A handsome maple, particularly attractive in autumn with its red fruits. Caucasus, Turkey, Iran. Introduced 1866.

Acer triflorum

Kom.

A deciduous, medium-sized tree, to 15m (50ft) in the wild, less in cultivation. This species has light brown, deeply fissured, shaggy bark and sharply acute, small, dark brown winter buds. Papery leaves consist of three leaflets on each stalk. The leaflets are ovate to oblong-lanceolate with untoothed or slightly coarsely toothed margins. They are wedge-shaped at the base. The upper surface is deep green, hairy at first, then smooth; the lower surface is pale green with some hairs. Clusters of yellow flowers are followed by yellow-brown, densely hairy fruits. The nutlets with wings are 5–6cm (2–2½in) long and spread at right angles. A very handsome maple, the leaves turning scarlet in autumn. North China, Korea. Introduced 1923.

A. tschonoskii (p.90) is a small tree with 5-lobed leaves that are brilliant in autumn.

Acer truncatum
Bunge

A deciduous, small tree, to 10m (30ft) high, with greyish-brown, deeply fissured and shaggy bark and blackish-brown, ovate winter buds. The leaves are papery and 5–10cm (2–4in) long, slightly wider. They are truncate or nearly heart-shaped at the base and have 5–7 triangular-ovate, taper-pointed lobes with wide sinuses reaching halfway to the middle of the blade. The upper surface is deep lustrous green and smooth; the lower surface is pale green with some tufts of hair. Andromonoecious, yellowish-green flowers are produced in erect corymbs. The fruits are 6–7cm (2½–3in) long, spreading at obtuse or right angles. This is an elegant maple that is very attractive both when it is in flower and when the leaves turn scarlet and yellow in autumn. North China, Japan, Korea. Introduced 1881.

Acer tschonoskii
Maxim.

A deciduous, small tree, to 5m (15ft) high. The branchlets are purplish with some white markings, later greyish-brown and smooth; the winter buds are purplish and small. The rounded leaves are papery, 5–10cm (2–4in) long and wide, and deeply 5-lobed with heart-shaped bases. The lobes are ovate and tapering; the lateral ones are more triangular. They have wide sinuses and sharply toothed margins. The colour is bright green and smooth above, pale green with some reddish hairs when young below. The flowers are usually dioecious, rarely monoecious; they are yellowish-green and appear in racemes. Pale brown fruits have curved wings; nutlets with wings are 2.5–3cm (1–1¼in) long, spreading at obtuse angles. A very attractive maple with brilliant autumn tints. This maple is similar to *A. micranthum* but larger in all its parts (see p.71). Japan. Introduced 1902.

Acer turkestanicum
Pax (*A. platanoides* subsp. *turkestanicum* (Pax) P. C. de Jong)

A deciduous, medium-sized tree, to 15m (50ft) high. This species has grey and smooth bark and reddish winter buds. The large leaves, 10–25cm (4–10in) across, a little less in length, are 5–7-lobed and heart-shaped at the base. The lobes are triangular-tapering with narrow sinuses. The upper surface is bright glossy green; the lower surface is lighter with some tufts of white hairs. Bears corymbs of yellowish-green flowers followed by yellowish-brown fruits, 5–7cm (2–3in) long and spreading almost at right angles. Turkestan and northeast Afghanistan.

Acer ukurunduense
Trautv. & C. A. Mey.

A small, deciduous tree, to 10m (30ft) high and often multi-trunked. The bark is yellowish- or blackish-brown and roughish; the winter buds are reddish-crimson, long, pointed and densely yellow-woolly. Roundish, papery leaves, 7–12cm (3–5in) long, usually have five ovate, taper-pointed lobes with narrow sinuses reaching two-thirds of the way to the middle of the blade. The margins are coarsely toothed. The upper surface is deep green; the lower surface is paler with yellowish hairs especially on the veins. The flowers are dioecious; they are yellowish-green and are in terminal racemose panicles. Yellowish-brown fruits are produced in erect racemes; nutlets with wings are 1.5–2cm (½–¾in) long and spread erectly. A handsome maple with attractive autumn tints. Manchuria, Korea, Japan, . Introduced 1831.

Acer velutinum
Boiss. (*A. insigne* Boiss. & Buhse)

A deciduous, large tree, to 23m (75ft) or more high, with smooth, light brown bark and large, blackish-brown winter buds. Leaves, 7–15cm (3–6in) wide, slightly less in length, have 3–5 ovate lobes with wide sinuses cut one-third of the way to the middle of the blade. They are heart-shaped at the base and the margins are coarsely saw-toothed. The upper surface is dark green; the lower surface is paler with dense, pale brown hairs. Flowers are yellowish-green and produced in erect corymb-like panicles. They are followed by brown, downy fruits; nutlets with wings are 5–6cm (2–2½in) long, spreading at an angle of 90–120 degrees. Caucasus, Iran. Introduced 1873.

var. glabrescens This variety has leaves that are smooth and glaucous beneath.

var. vanvolxemii (Masters) Rehder 1938 This variety has larger leaves, up to 20cm (8in) across, that are somewhat glaucous beneath with some hairs on the veins.

Acer villosum

Wall. (*A. sterculiaceum* Wall. subsp. *sterculiaceum*)

A deciduous, medium-sized tree, to 14m (45ft) or more, with dark brown bark, stout branchlets and acute, dark brown winter buds with numerous scales. The 3–5-lobed leaves are papery, 14–20cm (5½–8in) across and about as long. The lobes are narrowly triangular and taper-pointed. They are forward-pointing with narrow sinuses, cut almost to the middle of the blade. The base is heart-shaped and the margins irregularly toothed. They are bright green above, paler beneath; both surfaces are hairy when young, the lower surface always has some tufts of hairs at the axil of the veins. Dioecious, yellowish-green flowers appear in slender racemes. The fruits are stout, brownish-yellow and hairy; nutlets with wings are 3.5–5cm (1½–2in) long, spreading at right angles. A handsome maple. Himalayas.

Acer wilsonii

Rehder (*A. campbellii* subsp. *wilsonii* (Rehder) P. C. de Jong)

A deciduous, medium-sized tree, to 12m (40ft) high, with green branchlets, later dark brown and smooth. The winter buds are small and yellowish-brown with six scales; they are slightly shaggily hairy. Papery leaves, 7–12cm (3–5in) long, are 3-lobed, occasionally with two additional basal lobes and rounded at the base. The lobes are triangular-ovate with tapering points and untoothed margins; they are forward-pointing, bright green above, dull beneath with some white hairs on the vein axils. The flowers are andromonoecious and yellowish-green with white petals; they are borne in hairless panicles. Brownish-yellow fruits have strongly convex nutlets up to 3.5cm (1½in) long, spreading horizontally. An elegant maple. China. Introduced 1907.

Acer × zoeschense

Pax (*A. campestre* × *A. lobelii*)

A deciduous, medium-sized, rounded tree, to 15m (50ft) high, with greyish and fissured bark; the winter buds are dark purple. Leaves are 7–12cm (3–5in) long with five ovate and blunt lobes; the wide sinuses are cut to almost halfway to the middle of the blade. The leaves are heart-shaped at the base and the margins are untoothed. The upper surface is reddish-purple when young, later glossy green with some purple overtones, paler beneath with some hairs. Yellowish-green flowers appear in corymb-like panicles. The fruits are green, tinted rose and have flat nutlets. The nutlets with wings are 5.5–6cm (2¼–2½in) long, spreading almost horizontally. Garden origin c1880.

A-Z OF JAPANESE MAPLES

A selection of Japanese Maples (forms of *A. palmatum*) which are described in the following groups:

A The Palmate Group

These have foliage that is similar to that of the species *A. palmatum*. A1 Green-leaved; A2 Red-leaved.

B The Dissectum Group

This group has neatly divided leaves, the lobes being cut to the base and pinnately dissected and/or doubly pinnately dissected; the margins are toothed or saw-toothed. B1 Green-leaved; B2 Red-leaved.

C The Deeply Divided Group

The foliage of this group of cultivars is composed of 5, 7 or 9 lobes which are deeply cut to the base of the leaf. They are cultivars of *A. palmatum* subsp. *matsumurae*. C1 Green-leaved; C2 Red-leaved.

D The Linearilobum Group

The leaves of this group have long, narrow lobes, deeply cut to the base of the leaf.

E The Dwarf Group

Comprising slow-growing or compact cultivars. In Japanese horticulture, known as the Yatsubusa Group.

F The Variegated Group

All the cultivars in this group have variegated foliage.

G The Group for Foliage Effect

The cultivars in this group have special features –

which is either a variety of foliage or bark colour or texture.

'Aka Shigitatsusawa'

F

A tall shrub, to 3m (10ft) high. The leaves are 7–9-lobed, the lobes cut up to two-thirds of the way to the middle of the blade. They are green with strong overtones of pink or red, the veins clearly marked out. An attractive maple.

'Akegarasu'

A2

A large, upright shrub, to 4m (12ft) high. The leaves are large with up to 7 lobes, the lobes ovate-acute and cut halfway to the centre of the blade. Margins are lightly toothed. The leaves are rich reddish-purple in spring, later more dull red. A good cultivar.

'Aoba-jo'

E

A dwarf shrub, to 1m (3ft). The leaves are 5-lobed, the lobes ovate and taper-pointed. They are dark green, turning yellow in autumn.

A. *palmatum* 'Aoyagi'.

'Aoyagi'

A1

An upright shrub, to 3m (9ft) high. The leaves are 7-lobed, the lobes ovate-lanceolate, cut about halfway to the centre of the blade, long and tapering; the margins are saw-toothed. They are bright green; yellow in autumn. An attractive maple with notable green bark. 'Sango-kaku' (p.109) is a counterpart with red bark.

'Aratama'

E

A handsome, dwarf shrub, to 1m (3ft) high. The leaves are 6–7cm (2½–3in) long, 5–7-lobed, the lobes ovate-lanceolate, cut almost to the centre of the leaf; the margins are sharply toothed. The leaves are bright red.

'Asahi-zuru'

F Rising sun maple

A vigorous, upright shrub, to 3m (10ft) high. The foliage is green with sharply defined and clear variegations, some leaves being entirely white, some green with only a fleck of white. The leaves are 3.5cm (1½in) long and 3.5–6cm (1½–2½in) wide, 5-lobed, the lobes broad-ovate with wide sinuses, not deeply cut; finely toothed margins. A handsome maple, and hardy.

'Atropurpureum'

A2

An attractive maple, to 5m (15ft) high. The leaves are 5–7-lobed, the lobes ovate and taper-pointed, cut halfway to the centre of the leaf blade; the margins are lightly toothed. The foliage is dark purple in spring and summer, and scarlet in autumn.

'Aureum'

A1

An upright shrub, to 2.5m (8ft) high. The foliage is light yellow with red margins in spring, becoming light green, then turning yellow in autumn. The leaves are 5–7-lobed, the lobes ovate-lanceolate, taper-pointed, cut one-third of the way to the centre of the blade; the margins are finely toothed. The branchlets and stalks are bright red. A handsome maple.

A. *palmatum* 'Asahi-zuru'.

'Azuma-murasaki'

C2

A large shrub, to 5m (15ft) high. The leaves are 5–7-lobed, the lobes ovate-lanceolate, taper-pointed, cut to the base of the leaf; the margins are sharply toothed. The upper leaf surface is dark purple in spring, later becoming purplish with an undertone of green. The underside of the leaf is always green, until autumn when both sides are scarlet. An attractive maple.

'Beni-kagami'

('The Red Mirror')

C2

A handsome, large shrub, to 3m (10ft) high, with pendent branches. The leaves are 7-lobed, the lobes ovate-lanceolate and long-tapering, each lobe deeply cut to the base of the leaf; the margins are lightly toothed. The foliage is purplish-red in spring and summer, scarlet in autumn.

'Beni-komachi'

('A Beautiful Red-headed Little Girl') E

An elegant, dwarf maple, to 1m (3ft) high. The foliage is bright crimson in spring, turning greenish-red in summer and scarlet in autumn. The leaves are 5-lobed and the lobes are lanceolate, spreading at a wide angle and turning sideways. Each lobe is cut to the base of the leaf. The margins are irregularly toothed.

'Beni-maiko'

('Red Dancing Girl')

E

A beautiful, dwarf maple, to 1m (3ft) high. The foliage is scarlet in spring, but greenish-red with red veins in summer, and scarlet in autumn. The leaves are small and irregular with five ovate lobes, each lobe cut to the middle of the blade, short and taper-pointed, tending to curve sideways.

'Beni-schichihenge'

F

An upright shrub, to 1.8–2.2m (6–7ft) high. The foliage is bright green with pinky-orange markings and whitish margins, some leaves are predominently pinky-orange, some are basically green with a few pink mark-

A. *palmatum* 'Beni-schichihenge'.

ings. They are variable in size and shape, usually 5–7-lobed, the lobes ovate, taper-pointed; the margins are lightly toothed. A very beautiful maple.

'Beni-shidare'
('Red Cascading')
B2

A mushroom-shaped shrub, to 1.2m (4ft) high. The foliage is purple-red in the spring turning bronzy in the summer, and not retaining the deep red. It is scarlet in autumn. The leaves are 7-lobed, the lobes ovate-lanceolate narrowing to the midrib at the base. The tip is taper-pointed and the margins delicately, finely and deeply cut, giving a lacy, fern-like appearance. A very desirable maple.

'Beni-tsukasa'
E

An attractive, shrubby maple, to 1.5m (5ft) high. The remarkable foliage is bright yellow-red in spring, with pink and red undertones, and scarlet in autumn. The leaves are 5-lobed, the lobes ovate-lanceolate, long-tapering with wide sinuses. They are cut to the base of the leaf. The central lobe is forward-pointing, the side lobes twisting sideways.

'Bloodgood'
A2

A strong-growing shrub, reaching 5m (15ft) high, with dark purple foliage that turns scarlet in autumn. The leaves are large, up to 12cm (5in) wide, and 5–7-lobed. The lobes are broad-ovate, taper-pointed, with wide sinuses and cut to one-third of the way to the centre of the blade; the margins are lightly toothed. An attractive maple with good colour and notable red fruits in autumn.

'Burgundy Lace'
C2

A notable maple making a large shrub or small tree, to 3.5–4m (12–13ft) and spreading to 5m (15ft) across, with dark purple-red foliage. The leaves are 5–7-lobed, the lobes lanceolate, taper-pointed, each cut to the base of the leaf; the margins are saw-toothed. A hardy and beautiful maple.

'Butterfly'
F

An upright, small tree, to 4m (12ft) high, having attractive light green foliage with flecks of cream or white. In spring the leaves are often edged in pink. They are 5-lobed, the lobes ovate-lanceolate, taper-pointed, each cut two-thirds of the way to the base of the blade; the margins are coarsely toothed. A dainty maple with attractive autumn colour, the white areas becoming deep scarlet.

'Chirimen-nishiki'
('A Colourful Type of Paper')
F

An attractive maple, to 1.8–2.2m (6–7ft) high. The unusual leaves are 5-lobed, the lobes linear-lanceolate, long-tapering; the margins are coarsely toothed. The foliage is basically green, sometimes with some white markings.

'Chishio Improved'
G

A shrubby maple with a twiggy habit and growing to 3–4m (10–12ft) high. The foliage is intense crimson when unfolding in spring. The leaves are 5-lobed, ovate-lanceolate and long-tapering. They have wide sinuses and are cut to two-thirds of the way to the base

A. *palmatum* 'Chitoseyama'.

of the blade; the margins are finely toothed. This is a very handsome maple, that is beautiful in spring and then again in autumn when the leaves turn scarlet. It prefers some shelter in the garden.

'Chitoseyama'

C2

A tall, rounded shrub, to 2.7m (9ft) high. The foliage is rich crimson becoming greenish and scarlet in autumn. Leaves 7-lobed, ovate, long-tapering, the basal lobes much smaller; the margins are sharply saw-toothed. An elegant maple.

'Coonara Pygmy'

E

A neat, dwarf maple, 1m (3ft) high, with bright green foliage, turning orange in autumn. Leaves variable – small on older wood, but larger on younger wood – 5-lobed, lobes ovate with wide sinuses and saw-toothed margins. A good plant for a rock garden. Originated in Australia.

'Corallinum'

E

A choice, dwarf maple, slowly growing to 1.5m (5ft) high, with very striking shrimp-pink leaves when unfolding in the spring, turning green in the summer and scarlet in autumn. The leaves are 5-lobed, the lobes ovate and taper-pointed with narrow sinuses and saw-toothed margins.

A plant under this name that came from the Netherlands is growing much more robustly and making a larger plant.

'Crimson Queen'

B2

This maple, which belongs in the Dissectum Group, makes a rounded, mound-shaped plant growing up to 1.2m (4ft) high. It has rich purple-red foliage, turning scarlet in autumn. The leaves are 7-lobed, the lobes ovate-lanceolate, attenuate to the mid-rib at the base, the tip taper-pointed, pinnately and finely dissected. A magnificent cultivar, holding its colour well throughout the growing season, even in full sun. Very beautiful in autumn.

PLATE V

Acer palmatum *Dissectum Group cultivars – autumn colours*

All leaves are shown at approximately half lifesize

A. *palmatum* 'Garnet'

A. *palmatum* 'Dissectum Atropurpureum'

A. *palmatum* 'Waterfall'

A. *palmatum* 'Seiryû'

'Deshôjô'

G

An upright maple, to 2.5m (8ft) high, with brilliant shrimp-pink foliage in spring, turning green in summer with tones of red and scarlet in autumn. Leaves are palmate with five ovate-lanceolate, taper-pointed lobes radiating from the centre; wide sinuses are cut to two-thirds of the way to the middle of the blade; the margins are saw-toothed. A choice cultivar.

'Dissectum'

('Dissectum Viride') B1

A well-known Japanese maple forming a rounded mushroom shape and growing to 1.2m (4ft) high. The foliage is green, turning yellow in autumn. Leaves, 6cm (2½in) long, are 7–9-lobed, the lobes are lanceolate and each one separates entirely to the base of the leaf, pinnately and finely dissected. A handsome maple, very elegant in autumn.

'Dissectum Atropurpureum'

B2

A handsome, mound-shaped maple, to 1.2m (4ft) high. The foliage is variable but usually reddish-purple. Leaves have 7–9 lanceolate lobes, each cut to the base of the leaf; the margins are deeply incised.

The name A. *palmatum* 'Dissectum Atropurpureum' covers a number of clones which vary in colour and quality. These include, for example, 'Beni-shidare' (p.94) and 'Ornatum', which closely resembles the description given above.

'Dissectum Flavescens'

B1

An attractive, mound-shaped maple, to 1.5m (5ft) high, with distinct yellow-green foliage, turning yellow in autumn. The leaves have seven ovate-lanceolate lobes, each deeply cut to the base of the leaf; the margins are deeply and coarsely cut.

'Dissectum Nigrum'

('Ever Red') B2

A choice cultivar of cascading habit in the Dissectum Group. Growing to 3m (10ft) high, it has striking spring foliage – unfolding purple-red leaves are covered with fine silvery hairs. It is also lovely in autumn when the foliage becomes rich scarlet. The leaves are 7cm (3in) long and have seven lanceolate lobes, each cut to the base of the leaf and pinnately and finely dissected.

A. *palmatum* Dissectum Group.

'Elegans'

C1

A vigorous maple, to 4m (12ft) high, with rich green foliage, turning rich scarlet in autumn, sometimes with some yellow. The leaves are 5–7-lobed, the lobes ovate, long-tapering with wide sinuses cut to the base of the leaf; the margins are saw-toothed. A choice plant, beautiful in autumn.

'Filigree'

B1

An attractive maple, 1.2–1.5m (4–5ft) high and in the Dissectum Group, the lace-like foliage having a delicate texture and turning rich yellow in autumn The leaves, 6cm (2½in) long, are 9-lobed. The lobes are ovate and long-tapering, each lobe cut to the base of the leaf and deeply and delicately incised; the margins of each incision are again finely toothed, making it doubly dissected and fern-like.

'Fireglow'

A2

A vigorous maple, to 2.7m (9ft) high. The foliage is rich purple-red, turning scarlet in autumn. The leaves have 5–7 ovate, taper-pointed lobes with saw-toothed margins. A handsome maple, similar to 'Bloodgood'.

'Garnet'

B2

A choice, bun-shaped maple, to 2m (6ft) high. The foliage is rich red-orange, turning scarlet in autumn. The leaves are 7–9cm (3–3½in) long and 5–7-lobed, the lobes are ovate-lanceolate, taper-pointed with wide sinuses, and cut to the base of the leaf; the margins are deeply and coarsely incised.

'Garyu'

E

A rare, compact, dwarf maple, 1m (3ft) high, with attractive light green foliage, that has a reddish overtone in spring. The small leaves have 3–5 lanceolate, taper-pointed lobes, spreading at a wide angle, reaching sideways; the margins are saw-toothed.

'Goshiki-kotohime'

E

An attractive, dwarf maple, to 1m (3ft) high, with rich green foliage, slightly flecked with cream or pink markings, pinkish in spring and scarlet in autumn. Leaves are 5-lobed, the lobes ovate-lanceolate, each lobe cut to the base of the leaf, taper-pointed; the margins are saw-toothed.

'Green Trompenburg'

C1

A large shrub or small tree, to 5m (15ft) high, with dark shiny green foliage turning yellow in autumn. The leaves have 5–7 convex lobes with inrolled edges.

'Hagoromo'

('Dress Worn by Japanese Angels') G

An upright, shrubby maple, to 2.2m (7ft) high, with feathery foliage that is dark green, turning yellow and orange in autumn. The stalkless leaves are 5-lobed, the lobes lanceolate, tapering at the base and tips. Each leaf twists and turns at a different angle. A striking maple with unusual foliage.

'Hanami-nishiki'

E

A dwarf maple, growing slowly to 1m (3ft). The foliage is orange-red in spring, later light green. The small leaves, 1cm (½in) long, consist of five ovate lobes with wide sinuses cut to the centre of the blade; the margins are finely toothed. A very choice, rare maple.

'Harusame'

F

An attractive maple, to 2.2m (7ft) high. The foliage is usually variegated with white, but this is not always apparent; it turns striking red with yellowish-brown markings in autumn. The leaves consist of five ovate, long-tapering lobes with narrow sinuses cut to the centre of the blade; the margins are saw-toothed.

'Hazeroino'

G

A variegated maple, growing slowly to 1.5m (5ft) high. The foliage is bright green with cream-coloured markings. Broad-ovate leaves have 2 or 4 small side lobes. They are taper-pointed with finely toothed margins.

A. *palmatum* 'Dissectum'.

A. *palmatum* 'Heptalobum'.

'Heptalobum'

A1

A strong shrub or small tree, to 5m (15ft) high, with bright green foliage turning scarlet in autumn. The leaves are 7–9-lobed with ovate, long-tapering lobes that have wide but not deeply cut sinuses; the margins are finely toothed. A handsome maple with good autumn colour.

'Hessei'

C2

A beautiful, strong maple, to 4m (12ft) high, with rich purple-red foliage turning bright crimson in autumn. The leaves, 7cm (3in) long, have seven forward-pointing, ovate-lanceolate, long-tapering lobes with narrow sinuses cut to the base of the leaf; the margins are saw-toothed.

'Higasayama'

F

An upright maple, to 4.25m (14ft) high, with variegated foliage that is especially attractive in spring when the young pale cream or yellowish unfolding leaves contrast with their bright crimson sheaths. The leaves mature bright green with cream margins with an overlay of pink becoming more green in summer; orange or scarlet in autumn. They are 7-lobed, the lobes lanceolate, taper-pointed with narrow sinuses cut to two-thirds of the way to the base of the blade of the leaf; the margins are saw-toothed.

'Ichigyôji'

A1

A strong-growing maple, to 5m (15ft) high. This cultivar has bright green foliage, turning yellow or orange in autumn.The leaves consist of seven ovate-lanceolate leaves with wide, deeply cut sinuses; the margins are finely toothed. An elegant maple similar to 'Ôsakazuki' but with different autumn colour.

'Inaba-shidare'

B2

A mushroom-shaped maple that belongs in the Dissectum Group, to 2m (6ft) high. The leaves are deep purple-red, turning bright crimson in autumn. They are 6–7cm (2½–3in) long with nine lanceolate lobes. They taper strongly at the base and the tip, and have deeply dissected margins. A very choice maple, very attractive in autumn and desirable for planting by water.

'Inazuma'

('The Thunderer') B2

A notable shrub, to 3m (10ft) high, with pendent branches. The foliage is deep purple-red, turning crimson in autumn. The leaves, 7–9cm (3–3½in) long, have 5–7 lobes. The lobes are ovate-lanceolate, long-tapering with narrow sinuses cut to the base of the leaf; the margins are finely toothed. Worthwhile planting in any group of maples.

'Issai-nishiki'

G Pine bark maple

An unusual, upright but shrubby maple, to 1m (3ft) high. The bark becomes rough and corky with age and the foliage is bright green, turning yellow in autumn. Palmate, 7-lobed leaves consist of two very small basal lobes and five larger ovate-lanceolate, taper-pointed lobes. The narrow sinuses are cut to the middle of the blade and the margins are strongly toothed.

'Kagiri-nishiki'

('Roseomarginatum') F

An open, shrubby variegated maple, to 4m (12ft) high. The deep green leaves have rose and cream margins. They are 5-lobed, the lobes lanceolate or lanceolate-ovate, long-tapering with wide sinuses cut two-thirds of the way to the base of the blade; many of the lobes turn inwards and are sickle-shaped. Margins are finely toothed. A choice cultivar, very attractive in autumn, the rose and cream areas becoming vivid crimson.

'Kamagata'

E

A neat, dwarf maple, to 1m (3ft) high, with foliage that is reddish in spring, later bright light green, and yellow and orange in autumn. The leaves are 3–5-lobed, the lobes are wide-spreading and cut to two-thirds of the way to the base of the blade. They are lanceolate, long-tapering with saw-toothed margins. The tip of each lobe curves gently downwards. A beautiful cultivar that is especially suitable for a rock garden.

'Karasugawa'

F

An unusual, upright maple, to 2.5m (8ft) high, with spectacular pink foliage in spring, turning green with some flecks of pink in summer, and scarlet in autumn. The leaves are 5-lobed, the lobes ovate-lanceolate with narrow sinuses, cut to two-thirds of the way to the base of the blade, and saw-toothed margins. This is a fragile maple and difficult to grow; it is probably best in a container where it can be given more care.

'Kasagi-yama'

C2

A strong-growing maple, to 2.7m (9ft) high, with unusual brick-red foliage that has tones of green, turning scarlet in autumn. The leaves are 7-lobed, the lobes radiating from the base of the blade. They are ovate-lanceolate and long-tapering; the sinuses are narrow and cut to the base of the blade and the veins are clearly marked out. The margins are finely toothed.

'Kashima'

E

A handsome, dwarf maple, to 1m (3ft) high. The rich green foliage turns yellow in autumn. The leaves consist of five wide-spreading lobes, cut to two-thirds of the way to the base of the leaf. They are ovate, long-tapering and have finely toothed margins. A good shrubby maple for a rock garden.

'Katsura'

E

A small maple, to 2.7m (9ft) high. This has splendid spring foliage, the leaves yellow-orange turning rich green in summer, then yellow and orange in autumn. The leaves are small with five ovate-lanceolate, long-tapering lobes. Each is cut to two-thirds of the way to the base of the blade. The margins are saw-toothed.

'Kihachijô'

A1

A strong-growing maple, to 4m (12ft) high, with green bark covered with a bluey bloom. The foliage is bright green, turning yellow-gold in autumn. The leaves are 5–6cm (2–2½in) long. They have 7–9 ovate, taper-pointed lobes that are not deeply cut, and doubly saw-toothed margins. A handsome cultivar.

'Kinran'

('Woven with Golden Strings') C2

A small, shrubby maple, to 2.7m (9ft) high. The foliage is a deep rich purple-red, with the mid-veins a contrasting bright green. It turns a beautiful golden-

A. *palmatum* 'Ichigyôji'.

crimson in autumn. The leaves are 7-lobed, the lobes ovate-lanceolate, cut to two-thirds of the way to the base of the blade. They are narrow at the base with taper-pointed tips and deeply toothed margins. This maple is not well known, but very attractive.

'Kinshi'

('With Golden Threads') A1

A small maple, to 2m (6ft) high, with bright green foliage turning orange-yellow in autumn. The leaves are 7-lobed.

'Kiri-nishiki'

B1

A strong, shrubby maple in the Dissectum Group, to 2.7m (9ft) high, the foliage is bright green, turning yellow in autumn. The leaves are 6cm (2½in) long and 7cm (3in) across. They have nine lanceolate lobes, tapering at the tips and bases. The margins are double-toothed. An elegant plant with cascading foliage.

A. *palmatum* 'Koto-no-ito'.

'Kiyohime'

E

An attractive, dwarf maple, to 1.2m (4ft) high. The bright green leaves are tinged beautifully with orange-red in spring, and turn yellow in autumn. They have five broad-ovate lobes, the centre one longer than the side ones. The sinuses are narrow and taper-pointed and are cut to two-thirds of the way to the base of the blade. The margins are sharply toothed.

'Koreanum'

A1

A sturdy maple, to 4m (12ft) high. The foliage is bright green, turning rich crimson in autumn. The leaves consist of five ovate-lanceolate, taper-pointed lobes, the centre lobe being longer than the side lobes. The sinuses are narrow and cut to the middle of the leaf blade; the margins are lightly toothed. This is an elegant maple.

A. *palmatum* 'Koreanum' is not, in reality, a true cultivar of A. *palmatum* but it is a variety that is found in Korea. There are some selected clones of this variety; one of these has been named 'Korean Gem', but it is very rare.

'Kotohime'

E

This is a dwarf maple, to 1m (3ft) high. The foliage is orange-red in spring, then bright green, becoming golden-yellow in autumn. The small leaves have five ovate, short-tapering lobes, the central one longer than the side ones, which are wide-spreading. The margins are deeply saw-toothed. A beautiful maple, deserving a place in the garden.

'Koto-no-ito'

D

An upright maple, to 2.7m (9ft) high, with green foliage, turning yellow in autumn, and bright green bark. The leaves are 5-lobed. When young the lobes are ovate-lanceolate, long-tapering; later they become linear-lanceolate. The young leaves have narrow sinuses, cut two-thirds of the way to the base of the blade, and sharply toothed margins; later the toothing is less noticeable. Often the young leaves and more mature leaves can be seen on the same plant, producing an unusual appearance.

A. *palmatum* 'Lutescens' and A. *palmatum* 'Heptalobum' in their full autumn glory.

'Kurabu-yama'
C1

A strong-growing, shrubby maple, to 2.7m (9ft) high, with reddish-brown foliage in spring, later becoming rich deep green then bright scarlet in autumn. The leaves have seven ovate lobes, each lobe cut two-thirds of the way to the base of the blade, with tapering tips and bases and saw-toothed margins. The lobes often overlap. This maple is little known, but very attractive.

'Linearilobum'
('Shina Buga Oka') D

A handsome maple, to 4m (12ft) high. The foliage is bright green, turning yellow in autumn. The leaves are 7-lobed, the lobes lanceolate-linear, like an outstretched hand; each lobe is cut almost to the base of the leaf and is long-tapering.

'Linearilobum Rubrum'
('Atrolineare') D

This maple is similar to 'Linearilobum', but the leaves are purplish-red, turning scarlet in autumn.

'Little Princess'
('Mapi-no-machihime') E

A handsome, dwarf maple, to 60cm (2ft) high and spreading to 1.5m (5ft) wide, densely branched. The foliage is bright green, turning yellow with tones of crimson in autumn. The leaves are 5–7-lobed. A very choice maple, always attracting attention.

'Lutescens'
A1

A sturdy maple, to 5m (15ft) high, with bright green leaves, turning rich yellow-gold in autumn. The leaves are 6–7cm (2½–3in) long and 7-lobed, the lobes ovate and taper-pointed, and cut halfway to the base of the blade; the margins are lightly toothed.

'Maiko'
A1

An interesting, shrubby maple, up to 2m (6ft) high, with bright green foliage, turning yellow in autumn. Variable leaves are 5–6cm (2–2½in) long and 5-lobed. The lobes spread at wide angles, the middle one is longer than the side ones; they are lanceolate to ovate, short-tapering, with deeply and irregularly toothed margins.

'Mama'

('Doing as One Pleases') A1

An unusual maple, 3–4m (10–12ft) high, with variable foliage – often no two leaves are the same. The foliage is bright green in summer, turning yellow in autumn. The leaves are 3- or 5-lobed; the lobes lanceolate-linear or ovate. The linear lobes spread at right angles and are deeply cut, while the broad-ovate leaves have narrow sinuses, cut to the middle of the blade. The margins are irregularly toothed or deeply saw-toothed.

'Matsukaze'

C1

An attractive, broad-spreading maple, to 4m (12ft) high, with spectacular bronze-red or purple-red foliage in spring, turning rich green in summer and scarlet in autumn. The leaves, 6–7cm (2½–3in) long, are 7-lobed; the lobes are ovate-lanceolate with tapering bases and tips. The margins doubly saw-toothed.

'Mikawa-yatsubusa'

E

A dwarf maple, to 1m (3ft) high. The foliage is bright green, turning yellow in autumn. The leaves overlay each other like the curtains on a stage; the outer ones have red tips. They are 7-lobed and 3.5–5cm (1½–2in) long. The lobes are ovate-lanceolate and long-tapering, each lobe cut to two-thirds of the way to the base of the blade; the margins are finely toothed. A choice cultivar, deserving a place in a rock garden.

'Momoiro-koya-san'

E

An exciting new cultivar introduced by Dick van der Maat Entcultures. The foliage is a bright peach colour, later turning delicate shades of pink, red, white, green and yellow; in the autumn it is orange-red. The leaves are palmate, 2.5–5cm (1–2in) wide and 5–7-lobed.

'Moonfire'

A2

A fine maple, to 5m (15ft) high. The foliage is rich dark purple-red, turning scarlet in autumn. The leaves, 6–7cm (2½–3in) long, are 5–7-lobed, the lobes ovate-lanceolate and long-tapering with narrow sinuses cut to two-thirds of the way to the base of the blade. The margins are saw-toothed.

'Mure-hibari'

C1

A handsome, strong, upright maple, to 4m (12ft) high. The foliage is green with overtones of red in spring, becoming green in summer, and yellow and crimson in autumn. The leaves consist of seven lanceolate, taper-pointed lobes, each cut almost to the base of the leaf; the margins are deeply saw-toothed.

'Muro-gawa'

A2

A strong-growing, shrubby maple, to 4m (12ft) high, with reddish-yellow foliage in spring, becoming deep green in summer, and yellow and crimson in autumn. The leaves, 7–9cm (3–3½in) long, are 7-lobed, the lobes ovate and long-tapering, and each one cut to the centre of the blade; the margins are saw-toothed.

'Murusaki-kyohim'

E

A delightful, dwarf maple, multi-branched and growing to 1m (3ft) high. The foliage is light yellow-green, with overtones of purplish-red in spring, becoming bright green in the summer and rich yellow in autumn. The leaves, 2.5–4cm (1–1½in) long, are 5-lobed, the central lobe longer than the side lobes. The lobes are ovate-lanceolate and taper-pointed with wide sinuses cut almost to the base of the leaf; the margins are saw-toothed.

'Nicholsonii'

C2

A splendid maple, to 2.7m (9ft) or so high and multi-branched. The foliage is reddish-purple in spring, turning rich green in summer and fiery scarlet in autumn. The 7-lobed leaves are 6–7cm (2½–3in) long. The three centre lobes are longer than the side lobes; they are forward-pointing, ovate-lanceolate and long-tapering with saw-toothed margins. Very beautiful in autumn.

'Nishiki-gawa'

G2 Pine bark maple

A bushy, upright maple, to 4m (12ft) high, with green bark later becoming roughish. The foliage is bright green, turning yellow in autumn. The leaves, 3.5–5cm (1½–2in) long, have seven ovate-lanceolate, long-tapering lobes and are cut over halfway to the centre of the blade; the basal lobes are very small; the margins are finely toothed.

'Nuresagi'
A2

A maple, to 5m (15ft) high, with rich dark purple foliage, turning scarlet in autumn. The leaves, 7–9cm (3–3½in) long, are 7-lobed, the long lobes spread outwards and are ovate-lanceolate and taper-pointed; the margins are finely saw-toothed. This maple has attractive bark with whitish striations.

'Ô-kagami'
('The Mirror') A2

A strong-growing maple, to 4m (12ft) high, with rich dark purple foliage, sometimes with tones of green in late summer, turning scarlet in autumn. The leaves have seven lobes which radiate outwards and are cut to two-thirds of the way to the base of the blade. They are ovate, long-tapering, with finely toothed margins.

'Okushimo'
G

An excellent maple, upright in habit and to 5m (15ft) high. The rich green foliage turns a splendid golden-yellow in autumn. The leaves are 5–7-lobed, the lobes lanceolate and sharply taper-pointed with wide sinuses cut to two-thirds of the way to the base of the blade. The margins are bluntly toothed and turn over inwards, like a tube. An unusual maple but very desirable.

'Omurayama'
A1

A beautiful maple, to 4m (12ft) high, one of the few with pendent branches. The bright green leaves turn vivid golden-crimson in autumn. They are 6–7cm (2½–3in) long and have seven ovate-lanceolate lobes with narrow sinuses cut almost to the base of the blade; the margins are neatly toothed.

'Orange Dream'
A1

A very desirable maple with yellow or yellowish-green foliage, turning bright yellow in autumn, and green bark. The leaves are 5–7-lobed. This unusual maple needs some shelter from the sun.

A. *palmatum* 'Ôsakazuki'.

'Oregon Sunset'
B2

A striking new cultivar, to 2m (6ft) high, with reddish or reddish-green foliage in summer, turning scarlet in autumn. The leaves consist of five lanceolate lobes with finely saw-toothed margins.

'Orido-nishiki'
F

An upright maple, to 5m (15ft) high. The variegated foliage is bright green with areas of white or cream – sometimes the leaf is entirely pink especially in spring. The bark is greenish-purplish with pink striations. The leaves, 5–6cm (2–2½in) long, are 5-lobed, the lobes wide-spreading, cut to the middle of the blade, lanceolate, long-tapering and with saw-toothed margins. A splendid plant, and one of the best variegated maples.

'Ôsakazuki'
A1

A lovely old cultivar, the best known of the Japanese maples. A large shrub or a small tree, to 5m (15ft) high, with bright green foliage in summer, turning brilliant scarlet-crimson in autumn. The large leaves, 7–9cm

(3–3½in) long, are palmate with seven lobes; the lobes are ovate and sharply taper-pointed with narrow sinuses; the margins are saw-toothed. Especially beautiful in autumn.

'Oshio-beni'
A2

A popular, strong-growing maple, to 5m (15ft) high and upright in habit. The foliage is orangy-red, becoming bright scarlet in autumn. The leaves, 7–9cm (3–3½in) long, have seven ovate lobes, cut to one-third of the way to the middle of the blade and long-tapering; the margins are sharply toothed.

'Ôshû-shidare'
C2

A small, round-headed tree, to 2.7m (9ft) high, with pendent branches. The foliage is dark purple-red, going scarlet in autumn. The leaves are ovate-lanceolate with seven lobes. The lobes spread outwards and are cut to the base of the leaf. They are narrow at the base while the tip is long-tapering and the margins are saw-toothed. This old and famous cultivar has long been a favourite in Japan.

'Otome-zakura'
A2

An interesting, small, bushy maple, to 2.5m (8ft) high, with attractive foliage that has pinky tints in spring, turns dark green in summer and is yellow and crimson in autumn. The leaves are 5-lobed.

'Peaches and Cream'
E

A small maple, to 2.5m (8ft) high, that originated in Australia. It has variegated foliage that is green with tones of pink and crimson but, unfortunately, it is not easy to establish and grow.

'Pendulum Julian'
B2

An elegant cultivar in the Dissectum Group, to 2.7m (9ft) high and with pendent branches. The foliage is deep purple-red becoming purple with tones of green

A. *palmatum* in autumn, its brilliant red foliage a perfect foil for the yellow-leaved maple behind.

A. *palmatum* 'Red Pygmy'.

late in summer, then scarlet in autumn. The leaves are 7–9cm (3–3½in) long and 7-lobed with deeply and attractively cut margins. The lobes are wide-spreading and lanceolate; they are very narrow at base and the tip is long-tapering. Very hardy.

'Pixie'
E

A dwarf, multi-branched maple, 1–1.2m (3–4ft) high. The 5-lobed leaves are small and dark purple-red, and turn scarlet in autumn. This is a fairly new introduction from the USA.

'Red Filigree Lace'
B2

This is a beautiful maple, 1.2m (4ft) or so high and belonging to the Dissectum Group. The deep purple-red leaves turn bright scarlet in autumn. They are 5–7-lobed and the lobes are pinnatifid, each pinna being very delicately cut to give a very lacy appearance. This is an outstanding cultivar.

'Red Pygmy'
D

An attractive mound-shaped maple, to 1.5m (5ft) high, in the Linearilobum Group. The foliage is reddish-purple in summer, turning scarlet in autumn. The leaves, 7–9cm (3–3½in) long, are 7-lobed; each lanceolate-linear lobe is wide-spreading and cut to the base of the leaf. The margins are lightly toothed. This excellent maple is becoming very popular.

'Rubrum'
A2

A strong-growing, upright cultivar, to 4m (12ft) high, with dark purplish-red foliage, turning scarlet in autumn. The leaves, 10–11cm (4–4½in) long, consist of seven ovate and taper-pointed lobes with wide sinuses cut to one-third of the way to the base of the blade; the margins are saw-toothed. This is an old cultivar.

'Rufescens'
A2

A nice plant, to 2.7m (9ft) high, with brownish-red foliage in spring, turning reddish with green tones in summer, and yellow and scarlet in autumn. The leaves consist of seven ovate, long-tapering lobes, cut to the middle of the blade; the margins are saw-toothed. This is not a strong-growing cultivar, but contrasts well with other maples.

'Ryuzu'

('Dragons Head') E

A very desirable, dwarf maple, to 1m (3ft) high. The leaves, which are tightly spaced and overlapping, are green with shades of pink in the spring, becoming light green in summer and scarlet in autumn. They are 5-lobed, the lobes ovate, long-tapering, wide-spreading and cut to two-thirds of the way to the base of the blade. The margins are saw-toothed.

'Sagara-nishiki'

F

An attractive cultivar, but rare, to 1.5m (5ft) high. The light green leaves are variegated with yellow. They consist of five ovate, taper-pointed lobes, cut to the middle of the blade; the margins are saw-toothed.

'Samidare'

A1

A strong-growing maple, to 4m (12ft) high, with large leaves, pinkish in spring but then bright green, turning yellow and crimson in autumn. The leaves are 6–7cm (2½–3in) long and have seven lobes, which are ovate, long-tapering, wide-spreading and cut to the middle of the blade; the margins are finely saw-toothed. This is a hardy cultivar and quick-growing.

'Sango-kaku'

('Senkaki') G1

A very popular cultivar with an upright habit, to 5m (15ft) high. This tree has striking coral-pink bark and bright green foliage, turning golden-yellow with tones of red in autumn. The palmate leaves are 5–7-lobed, the lobes ovate and long-tapering; the margins are saw-toothed. This elegant cultivar is deserving of a place in every garden and is especially attractive in winter.

'Saoshika'

A1

An upright cultivar, to 2m (6ft) high, with roundish, bright green foliage turning yellow and crimson in autumn. The leaves, 5–6cm (2–2½in) long, have 5–7 ovate, long-tapering, wide-spreading lobes, cut to the middle of the blade. The margins are saw-toothed. Attractive when the sun is behind the leaves and in the winter when the silvery bark is notable.

'Sazanami'

C1

An attractive maple, to 2m (6ft) high. The foliage is light red with overtones of green in spring, turning rich green in summer and yellow in autumn. The leaves are 3.5–5cm (1½–2in) long and 7-lobed. The lobes are ovate-lanceolate, long-tapering and cut almost to the base of the leaf. They are forward-pointing and have saw-toothed margins. Not yet very common.

'Seigen'

E

A dwarf maple, to 1m (3ft) high, with fiery crimson foliage in spring, turning light green in summer and yellow in autumn. The leaves are small, 2.5–4cm (1–1½in) long and 5-lobed. The lobes are lanceolate and long-tapering. They are wide-spreading and cut

A. *palmatum* 'Sango-kaku'.

two-thirds of the way to the base of the blade; the margins are saw-toothed. A very choice maple, especially good in spring.

'Seiryû'
B2

A most attractive cultivar in the Dissectum Group, unusual for its upright, vase-like shape and because it grows to 2.5m (8ft) or more. The foliage is bright green in summer, turning yellow or scarlet in autumn; the bark is green. The leaves, 3.5–5cm (1½–2in) long, are 7-lobed, the lobes pinnately dissected and attractively cut. This is a valuable addition to the group of Japanese maples, being hardy and growing in all soils. There are two clones, one colours yellow in the autumn, while the other turns scarlet, like a bonfire.

'Sekimori'
B1

A good form in the Dissectum Group making a mound-shaped plant, to 2.2m (7ft) or more. The foliage is a beautiful blue-green, turning golden-yellow in autumn; the bark is green with white striations. The leaves, 7–9cm (3–3½in) long, are 9-lobed, the lobes pinnatifid and finely cut. A strong, hardy plant.

A. palmatum 'Seiryû'.

'Sekka-yatsubusa'
E

A dwarf cultivar, to 1m (3ft) high with bright green foliage that has reddish tones in spring and turns yellow in autumn. Small leaves, 2.5–4cm (1–1½in) long, are 5-lobed, with very small basal lobes. They are ovate-lanceolate, long-tapering, wide-spreading and cut to two-thirds of the way to the base of the blade; the margins are saw-toothed. 'Yatsubusa' means 'dwarf' and this delightful maple is very desirable as a specimen for a rock garden.

'Shaina'
A1

A most attractive tree, usually to 3m (10ft) or so high, but sometimes more. The foliage is a good reddish-purple, turning scarlet in autumn. The leaves are 5-lobed, the centre lobe shorter than the other lobes. They are ovate, deeply cut and taper-pointed with saw-toothed margins. This maple is now becoming better known and is much sought after. It is a sport of 'Bloodgood', as shown by the cut-back central lobe. A very choice and desirable maple.

'Sherwood Flame'
C2

A sturdy maple, to 4m (12ft) high, the foliage a rich reddish-purple, turning scarlet in autumn. The leaves, 7–9cm (3–3½in) long, consist of seven ovate-lanceolate, long-tapering lobes that are not wide-spreading but are cut to the base of the leaf; the margins are saw-toothed. An excellent garden plant.

'Shigitatsu-sawa'
('Reticulatum') F

An open shrub up to 4m (12ft) high. The light green or yellowy-green leaves are strongly veined with dark green; they turn scarlet in autumn. They are 6–7cm (2½–3in) long with 7–9 lobes, the lobes ovate and long-tapering. They point outwards and are cut to one-third of the depth of the blade; the margins are saw-toothed. The contrast of the leaf colours is very attractive. It requires some protection from the sun.

A. palmatum 'Shaina'.

'Shigure-bato'

A2

A slow-growing, upright maple, reaching 2m (6ft). The foliage is green, with striking tones of red in spring, and turns yellow to crimson in autumn. The leaves are 5–6cm (2–2½in) long and have seven ovate-lanceolate, long-tapering lobes, very narrow at the base, pointing outwards and cut to the base of the leaf. The margins are deeply saw-toothed, giving the leaf a feathery look. An elegant maple.

'Shinonome'

C2

An upright cultivar, to 2.7m (9ft) high, with foliage that has bright reddish tones in the spring, later becomes green with overtones of red, and then turns scarlet in autumn. The leaves, 5–6cm (2–2½in) long, consist of seven ovate-lanceolate lobes, cut to two-thirds of the depth of the blade. They are long-tapering, the three central lobes are forward-pointing and the margins are saw-toothed.

'Shishigashira'

('Ribesifolium') G1

An attractive and unusual maple with an upright habit, usually to 2.7m (9ft) high, although sometimes larger. The bright green leaves are packed closely together on the end of the branches giving this maple a stubbly look. They turn scarlet in autumn. They are 3.5–5cm (1½–2in) long and 7-lobed; the lobes are ovate-lanceolate, sharply taper-pointed and cut almost at the base of the leaf; the margins irregularly cut and crinkled. This is a beautiful cultivar that always attracts attention and certainly deserves a place in a collection of maples (see p.112).

'Shôjô-nomura'

C2

This cultivar grows to 4m (12ft) high and has pendent branches. The foliage is a good purple-red in early spring, with undertones of green in the summer, and turning scarlet in autumn. The leaves, 5–6cm (2–2½in) long, consist of seven ovate lobes that are wide-spreading and cut to the base of the stalk; they are narrow at the base and tip and have saw-toothed margins.

'Stella Rossa'

B2

A new cultivar in the Dissectum Group and making a round-headed shrub, to 1.2m (4ft) high. The leaves are dark reddish-purple, turning scarlet in autumn. They consist of seven pinnatifid and finely dissected lobes.

'Sumi-nagashi'

C2

A large-leafed maple, strong-growing, upright and to 4m (12ft) high. The foliage is reddish-purple in spring becoming dark purple in summer, scarlet in autumn. Leaves, 7–9cm (3–3½in) long, have seven ovate-lanceolate, spreading lobes, cut to the leaf base. They are narrow at the base and the tip, with saw-toothed margins. A strong-growing cultivar with good colour tones.

'Tamahime'

E

An attractive maple, to 1.5m (5ft), with small, bright green leaves, turning yellow and scarlet in autumn. They are 2.5–4cm (1–1½in) long and 5-lobed, the lobes ovate-lanceolate; the central lobe is longer than the side lobes. They are wide-spreading and cut almost to the base of the leaf; the margins are saw-toothed. Ideal for a spot in the rock garden or as a focal point.

'Tamukeyama'

B2

A beautiful maple, 1m (3ft) high, with cascading branches and dark purple foliage. The leaves are pinnately and finely dissected with 7–9 lobes.

'Tana'

A1

An upright, strong-growing cultivar, to 4m (12ft) high with light yellowish-green foliage, bright yellow and red in autumn. The leaves consist of 5–7 ovate, taper-pointed lobes spreading at a wide angle and cut to the middle of the blade; the margins are lightly toothed.

'Toyama-nishiki'

F

A variegated cultivar, to 1m (3ft) high but not strong-growing. The leaves are purplish- or greenish-red with pink and white markings. They are 7–9-lobed, the lobes being doubly dissected, pinnatifid and lacy in appearance.

A. *palmatum* 'Shishigashira' (p.111).

'Trompenburg'

C2

A strong-growing, round-headed shrub, making 4m (12ft) high. The rich dark purple foliage turns scarlet in autumn. The leaves, 7–9cm (3–3½in) long, have 7–9 lanceolate lobes that are wide-spreading and cut to the base of the leaf. The margins, which are finely saw-toothed, are flat when young but later rolled over like a tube. This very popular and unusual maple has a good form and is attractive in autumn (see p.115).

'Tsuchi-gumo'

A1

A delightful, semi-dwarf cultivar, to 2m (6ft) high. The foliage is reddish when it first emerges in spring, later turning bright green and, in autumn, crimson and bright yellow. The leaves, 2.5–4cm (1–1½in) long, are 5–7-lobed; the lobes are ovate-lanceolate and not wide-spreading, and they are cut to two-thirds of the way to the base of the blade. The margins are saw-toothed. This is an excellent maple for a rock garden.

'Tsukubane'

C2

An upright cultivar, to 4.25m (14ft) high, with purple-red foliage, lighter in spring, bright scarlet in autumn. The leaves, 6–7cm (2½–3in) long, are 7-lobed; the lobes are ovate, long-tapering, not wide-spreading, and cut to two-thirds of the way to the middle of the blade. The margins are finely saw-toothed. Not widely known, but has good colour tones.

'Tsukushi-gata'

A2

This is an attractive cultivar, growing to 2.7m (9ft) high and making a round shrub. The foliage is rich deep purple-red in spring and summer, turning scarlet in autumn. The leaves, 7–9cm (3–3½in) long, are 7-lobed. The lobes are ovate and not wide-spreading; they are cut to about halfway to the centre of the blade. The basal lobes are small and the margins are saw-toothed. This maple also produces showy fruits in autumn.

'Tsuma-beni'

A1

A small maple of roundish shape, to 2m (6ft) high. Its outstanding feature is the light green leaves with purplish-red tips, turning scarlet in autumn. They are 6–7cm (2½–3in) long and 5–7-lobed, the lobes ovate and long-tapering, not wide-spreading, and cut to one-third of the way to the base of the blade; the margins are saw-toothed. An attractive cultivar with unusual foliage and notable spring colours.

'Ukigumo'

('Floating Cloud') F

An outstanding variegated cultivar, slowly growing to 2m (6ft) high and making a shrubby plant. The leaves are green with white and pink markings. They are 3.5–5cm (1½–2in) long and 5-lobed, the lobes ovate-lanceolate, wide-spreading and cut almost to the base of the leaf; the margins are saw-toothed. This is becoming a very popular cultivar, the soft colours subtly blending into each other.

'Umegae'

A2

A semi-dwarf cultivar, to 2m (6ft) high and roundish in habit. The foliage is bright purplish-red, turning scarlet in autumn. Small leaves, 3.5–5cm (1½–2in) long, are 7-lobed. The lobes are ovate, long-tapering, not wide-spreading, and cut to two-thirds of the way to the base of the blade. Margins are saw-toothed. This is a nice maple, but not fast growing.

'Utsu-semi'

A1

A beautiful cultivar, with broad, bold leaves, making a round shrub or small tree to 2.7m (9ft) high. Foliage is bright green, turning scarlet in autumn. The leaves are 7–9cm (3–3½in) long and 7-lobed, the lobes ovate, short-tapering, not wide-spreading, and cut to one-third of the way to the base of the blade; the basal lobes are small and the margins are saw-toothed. A fine maple with foliage that contrasts well with other maples.

'Versicolor'

F

A variegated cultivar, to 4m (12ft) high. Leaves are bright green with flecks of white or pink, branchlets green. They have 5–7 ovate, long-tapering lobes that are not deeply cut and have saw-toothed margins. A nice maple.

'Villa Taranto'

D

An excellent maple, roundish in shape and to 2m (6ft) high. The foliage is green with pink overtones, turning yellow in autumn. Leaves are 7–9cm (3–3½in) long with five linear lobes that are wide-spreading and cut to the base of the leaf; the centre lobes are longer than the side lobes and the margins are untoothed. A very attractive cultivar with a good colour effect.

'Volubile'

A1

An upright cultivar, reaching to 4m (12ft) high. The leaves are bright green, turning brilliant yellow and scarlet in the autumn. They are 3.5–5cm (1½–2in) long and palmately 7-lobed. The lobes are ovate, long-tapering, wide-spreading and cut to the middle of the blade; the margins are lightly toothed. A very beautiful maple, especially for its handsome foliage and autumn colour.

'Wabito'

G1

An attractive small, shrub-like plant, to 1.2m (4ft) high. It has unusual foliage which is green with marginal tones of red, turning scarlet in autumn. Leaves are 3.5–5cm (1½–2in) long and 3–5-lobed. The lobes are lanceolate, wide-spreading and cut to the base of the leaf; the margins are coarsely saw-toothed.

'Wakehurst Pink'

E

A small maple, to 2m (6ft) high, making an open-branched shrub. The foliage is green with areas of pink. The leaves consist of seven lanceolate lobes.

'Waterfall'

B1

A beautiful maple in the Dissectum Group, to 1.5m (5ft) high and making a roundish shape. The foliage is bright green, turning golden and scarlet in autumn. The leaves are large, 9–11cm (3½–4½in) long, with 7–9 lobes. The lobes are pinnatifid, very narrow at the base

A. palmatum 'Trompenburg' (p.113).

and long-tapering. This maple has good colour tones and is very striking in autumn.

'Wou-nishiki'

C2

An upright maple reaching 2.7m (9ft) high. The foliage is green with reddish tones in the spring, later bright green, then scarlet in autumn. The 7-lobed leaves are 3.5–5cm (1½–2in) long. The lobes are ovate-lanceolate, pointing outwards and cut to the base of the leaf; the margins are deeply saw-toothed.

'Yezo-nishiki'

A2

An upright maple, to 5m (15ft) high, with reddish-purple foliage, becoming scarlet in autumn. The leaves, 5–6cm (2–2½in) long, are 7-lobed, the lobes ovate, long-tapering, not wide-spreading, cut to the middle of the blade; the margins are finely saw-toothed. This is an attractive cultivar with good colour and form.

'Yubae'

F

A maple, to 4m (12ft) high, with dark purple foliage and beautiful silvery bark. The leaves are 7-lobed, the lobes ovate-lanceolate, taper-pointed, not wide-spreading, and cut to the base of the leaf. The basal lobes are smaller and the margins are deeply saw-toothed. The late J. D. Vertrees described this maple as having a reddish-purple foliage with crimson variegations. However, none of the plants in cultivation are showing any variegation. Nevertheless, the form here is a desirable maple with good colour.

'Yûgure'

(Twilight) A2

A nice cultivar with an upright habit, to 3m (10ft) high. The foliage is crimson when unfolding in spring, later reddish with tones of green, then reddish-crimson in autumn. The leaves, 6–7cm (2½–3in) long, are 7-lobed, the lobes ovate, long-tapering and wide-spreading; they are cut to two-thirds of the way to the base of the blade. The margins are saw-toothed.

6

CULTIVATION

Maples are adaptable plants and easy to cultivate. They can grow in all types of soil, although, not unnaturally in such a large genus, each species has its own preference. A well-drained loamy soil is, perhaps, ideal, but even this is just a broad generalization: in fact, there is a maple for almost any soil. They do not like wet feet, however, and, therefore, generally should not be planted in boggy conditions. An exception is *A. rubrum*, which will tolerate damper soil than most maples.

ACID OR ALKALINE?

All maples will grow on acid soil, but not all will grow on alkaline or chalky soils. Clay soils can have an overlay of acid soil or alkaline soil, so if you do not already know what your soil is like, it is advisable to test its pH before planting.

It is useful to know whereabouts in the world the species originated as this can tell you something about its soil preferences. For example, vast areas of China, including Hubei, from where many maples originate, have alkaline soil, and it follows that many maples from China are happy in similar soil in cultivation. By contrast, maples from Japan are usually lime-haters because much of Japan's soil is acidic in nature. However, in gardening no rule is without its exceptions: *A. forrestii*, a Chinese maple, hates alkaline soil and *A. carpinifolium*, from Japan, struggles on very alkaline soil and will not grow on chalk. Maples from the Himalayas, including *A. pectinatum* and *A. cordatum* prefer neutral to acid soil. The soil of Taiwan can generally be divided into two types: the older diluvial soil and the younger alluvial soil. In the cultivated areas of the island, the soil on elevated terraces belongs to the first group and is acidic; the soil in the central and southern parts of the island is mainly alkaline or neutral. Thus some Taiwanese maples tolerate alkaline soil. *A. kawakamii*, for example, is well-established in our garden, and does not seem to have suffered from being in soil that has a pH of 7.5.

Maples from Europe and the Caucasus are quite at home in either acid or alkaline soils. The United States has mostly acid soil and some maples from there are lime-haters. *A. pensylvanicum*, for instance, will not grow in a very alkaline soil. *A. rubrum* and *A. negundo* are more adaptable.

Curiously, and despite many comments to the contrary, the Japanese maples (*A. palmatum* and cultivars) do as well on acid soil as on alkaline soils. *A. palmatum* grows in both China and Japan. Many Japanese maples have grown happily in our garden for many years without any sign of stress.

SITE

Maples are not coastal plants; salt-laden winds blowing in from the sea will cause irreparable damage to their leaves. Japanese maples, whose leaves are more delicate than most, are particularly badly affected. However, I have seen the sycamore (*A. pseudoplatanus*) growing on the west coast of Scotland and it does fairly well, although some damage to the foliage does occur. My brother-in-law lives on the Isle of Man and was able, after a few years, to establish Japanese maples in his garden. They were planted in a valley along a stream so did get some protection from the salt winds.

The Japanese maple (*A. palmatum*) and its cultivars will do as well on acid as on alkaline soils.

A moderate amount of wind will not worry a maple. Some, for example A. *platanoides*, A. *cappadocicum* and A. *macrophyllum*, are forest trees and quite used to the varying and often hostile conditions found at forest margins. Of course, they will not thrive on the more exposed sites, such as the wilds of Dartmoor or peaks in Derbyshire, nor will they be happy in a wind tunnel, such as between two houses where the wind funnels through.

HARDINESS

Most maples are perfectly hardy. Those growing at a higher altitude in the wild (for example, A. *trautvetteri* and A. *platanoides*) can tolerate a great deal of cold, but a number of species are more tender and need either some winter protection or a frost-free garden. These include the evergreen maples, those from the Himalayas, Taiwan and southern China (A. *pentaphyllum*) as well as some from Hubei (A. *oblongum* and A. *flabellatum*). In mild climates, such as those experienced by southern England, most of these, including A. *paxii* and A. *albo-purpurascens*, require only the shelter of a polytunnel. More protection may be necessary in colder places.

A. *palmatum* 'Crimson Queen' is able to adapt to a wide variety of light conditions.

Japanese maples are remarkably tolerant and can grow in quite windy conditions. The homeland of these maples is the mountains of Japan and so they are also quite hardy. However, many of them have delicate foliage that can get damaged by cold winds so some protection is advisable.

SHADE OR SUNLIGHT?

Maples will not tolerate deep shade. The tree-like species prefer an open site. If they are planted too close to other trees, they will have to grow upwards in order to get to the light and will become long and spindly.

Many maples will adapt quite happily to an open site, even if in their native land they are found in woodland conditions. I have seen A. *palmatum* 'Crimson Queen' growing in North America and Italy, in sites where temperatures can reach 38°C (100°F) in the summer, but in each case the plants were in perfect condition and had not suffered at all from the hot sun.

Woodland conditions, however, and dappled shade are ideal for Japanese maples and some other shrubby maples. And this is a completely natural setting for these plants, as can be seen in the acer glades at Westonbirt Arboretum in Gloucestershire. Certainly, it is better to plant variegated cultivars of A. *palmatum* and other species in dappled shade as their leaves can easily burn in the sun. A. *palmatum* 'Orange Dream' also needs shade.

Of course, all these remarks do rely on circumstances being ideal. It must be remembered that any plant can take up to two years to adapt to its new conditions and establish itself, and during this time it may need some looking after and protection. Some plants can take even longer before showing any top growth as they will be putting down their roots first.

Autumn colour

In the autumn, maples come into their own, with many species being dressed in rich colours from scarlet to gold, or a mixture of the two. Autumn colour is due to a chemical change in the leaves and a combination of the remains of the chlorophyll grains and a substance called anthocyanin. The colour assumed by leaves depends on soil and air conditions and on the amount of moisture. If conditions are very dry in the autumn, then the colour will not last for long. After a frost, colours appear more intense, but the frost can check activity. It will also not be so good in very wet conditions.

BUYING AND PLANTING

When a maple is purchased it should be in good condition with a well-grown root system. If it has been raised in the open ground, then it should have a good rootball with plenty of fibrous young roots and it will transplant easily. Maples that have been grown in containers should look healthy, with the roots just filling the pot. A plant that has a tight rootball should be avoided as it has obviously been in its pot for a long time and is starved.

Planting

The preparation of the planting site is important, as a young plant that is given a good start will grow away well. A hole at least twice the size of the rootball should be dug out. Put some well-rotted farmyard manure or compost in the bottom. This should then be covered with some soil as the roots may be burnt (particularly by the farmyard manure) if they come into contact with it. Grass turves can also be used but are not recommended as leatherjackets, which will eat the roots, can be present in the grass. Make sure the turves are well chopped and that they are turned over so that the grassy side is face down. They should also be buried deeply.

Before planting, ensure the rootball is moist otherwise it may not take up moisture from the planting site immediately and may be slower to establish itself.

Planting the tree is often easier if it is done by two people. One person holds the tree upright while the other back-fills with soil mixed with some peat and leaf mould. Remember to spread out the roots in the bottom of the hole if you are planting a bare-root specimen. Bare-rooted trees must be planted to the same depth as they were in the nursery and potted specimens must be at the same level as the earth in the pot.

Once the hole is filled, the soil must be firmed in well around the newly-planted tree. This final step is very important as failures in planting ofen arise from insufficient firming – the roots can only draw water from soil that is pressed tightly against them.

Finally, spread a little fish, blood and bone or general fertilizer on top and water the tree again. If it has been planted in the autumn, no more watering should be necessary unless there is a particularly dry period. In the spring, however, more watering may be necessary, especially during a dry spell.

Staking

There are two schools of thought on staking plants. Some people argue that the young plant should be left without a stake so as to encourage its roots to go down and grip well, while others prefer a stake. My opinion is that with seedlings, or very young plants, a stake may not be necessary. However, with some plants, for example, standards, staking is better so as to avoid the soil around the rootball being disturbed. Plants that have been grafted should also be staked, so as to avoid the risk of the graft breaking. It is important that any ties are checked regularly so that they do not damage the bark of the young tree as it grows.

CONTAINERS

Many maples, especially the Japanese maples, are ideal for growing in containers as they have a fibrous root system and add an extra dimension to the garden. This gives you more flexibility about where it can be placed, or if its final site has not been determined, then the containerized maple can be moved around the garden during the summer so that the perfect position can be found.

With some exceptions, there are many containers that are suitable, provided that they have adequate drainage holes. Plastic containers are not always ideal, as in summer the soil can get too warm and in winter there is little or no protection against a frost. Wooden containers, too, can be attractive but may rot after a few years, and will then have to be replaced.

Cultivation in pots

The cultivation of Japanese maples in containers is quite easy, provided three important conditions are fulfilled. First, the compost should be light, friable and

PLATE VI

Acer buergerianum *and* A. negundo *and varieties*

All leaves are shown at approximately half lifesize
A. negundo 'Violaceum'
A. negundo 'Kelly's Gold'
A. negundo 'Flamingo'

Many maples, especially A. *palmatum* cultivars, will do very well in a pot and add an attractive focal point to a garden.

open, and well-drained. Secondly, there should be adequate drainage as Japanese maples do not like their feet in water. Thirdly, feeding should be done very carefully as Japanese maples do not like a lot of fertilizer.

The compost, when picked up, should fall away easily from the hand. If it is wet or sticky, it should not be used. Here, in the nursery, we use a compost made of (mostly) peat, forest bark and grit, to which some lime and fertilizer is also added. A soil-based compost, such as John Innes No.3, is quite satisfactory but it may be necessary to add some more forest bark and grit to make the texture more open and friable.

The leaves of a potted Japanese maple may burn at the edges, due to poor drainage or the soil being too wet. There is more risk of potted maples getting too much water in the winter as they need very little liquid during their dormant period. The problem is made worse if there are insufficient crocks in the bottom of the pot. If we have a specimen that is suffering from overwatering, we knock off all the wet compost and damaged roots until we get back to healthy ones and then we repot. The plant is then watered and left until the compost starts to dry before being watered again. Remember that, in spring, when the roots start to get active, potted maples will need more water, perhaps every day in the summer.

Maples do not need a lot of feeding. If, however, they look tired, they can be given a little foliar feed to encourage them. It is very important not to spray the plant when it is standing in full sun, otherwise the foliage may get burnt. Wait until the maple is shaded, perhaps in the evening, before spraying.

It is important to be sparing with the fertilizer. If too much is mixed in with the compost, then the roots of the maple may not be able to absorb it all and may be burnt rather than benefit. A maple that comes into leaf in the spring and then suddenly withers and dies is most probably suffering from this condition. Recently, I was asked to diagnose a problem in a Japanese maple that had withered and died. The owner had been dressing it with chicken pellets. These contain too much nitrogen and other adverse matter. The poor maple had simply been unable to manage and had given up the ghost.

If all the cultivation techniques described above are being followed but the maple still looks unhappy and is withering, its roots may have been eaten by vine weevil (see p.125). In this case, the maple should be washed clean of soil and replanted in new compost.

Well-established maples in containers can survive cold remarkably well. Young plants should be given some protection in really cold weather. They can be put into the conservatory or a garage or utility room. Alternatively, they can be wrapped in straw or bracken over the winter.

Repotting

Young maples should be repotted every year, and older maples, every two years. It is never a good idea to repot a maple that has been in a small container into a very large container, as it will make all root growth and no top growth. It is much better to increase the size of the pot gradually. If you want to achieve a certain effect by putting a young maple in a large pot, it is better to leave it in a smaller pot but then sink it into the earth of the larger pot. Lobelia or campanula can be planted around the edge.

PRUNING

Generally, maples do not need a lot of pruning. However, some may be necessary to improve their shape or to encourage healthy growth. Pruning is most likely to be required with young plants. Japanese maples, for example, grow fast when they are young and very often produce a single long shoot in one direction, which, if not pruned back, will produce an unsightly and unbalanced plant. Tree maples grown in the open ground should have a good leader. When they are young, some species may lose their leader and produce two side shoots instead; A. *davidii* often does this. If this has happened, one of the side shoots should be cut out and the other encouraged to form a good leader.

It is common for some maples, for example A. *palmatum* 'Dissectum', to produce a lot of dead wood, and this should always be pruned out to keep the plant tidy and healthy.

Finally, the roots of container-grown plants can be pruned so that they can be grown in pots of restricted sizes.

When to prune

Pruning is best carried out when the sap is falling in late summer and early autumn, although no harm will come if the operation is carried out even later, in mid-autumn. It is, in my view, better to complete pruning before the onset of cold weather. Light pruning of long, young branchlets can be carried out in spring.

If large branches are removed, then it may be a good idea to treat the cut with a wound sealant containing fungicide to prevent the entrance of disease or rot.

Some maples, for example A. *negundo* 'Flamingo', can be treated like willows. Their young branches, or the previous year's shoots, can be cut back in early spring. The resultant new growth will be in much brighter colours.

Maples such as A. *palmatum* 'Dissectum Ornatum' can be pruned to remove dead wood in late summer or early autumn.

A. *rubrum*, pictured here normal size, is among the many maples that can be grown as bonsai.

MAPLES AS BONSAI *by C. P. Ellis*

Bonsai are miniature trees in pots and the aim of growing them is to create an impression of nature in miniature. Plants with small leaves, exciting spring and autumn leaf colour, small flowers, small fruits, buttressed roots, impressive trunks and good branching and twigging characteristics lend themselves to being grown as bonsai. Many maples are suitable and can be grown as bonsai, either individually or in groups, in many ways that reflect nature, including the informal, slanting, windswept, multiple trunk and root over rock styles.

As well as their visual suitability, many maples are also vigorous growers, tolerant of pruning, of dry soil conditions and of air pollution. These characteristics make them good subjects for training as bonsai because in the early stages of making a bonsai, vigorous growth can be used to develop the structure of the miniature tree quickly and short internodal growth can be attained by keeping the plant relatively dry. Resistance to leaf damage is an advantage in a bonsai, although this is not a characteristic of all the A. *palmatum* cultivars. Correct bonsai training significantly reduces leaf size, too. With most maples, you can remove all the leaves in summer to force a second crop – two years' growth in one year – which will be smaller and produce better autumn colour and smaller leaves the following spring.

Acer species most suited to training for bonsai are: A. *buergerianum*, A. *campestre*, A. *ginnala*, A. *griseum*, A. *japonicum*, A. *monspessulanum*, A. *palmatum*, A. *rubrum*, A. *tenuifolium*, and their cultivars. A. *pseudoplatanus*, the sycamore, can also be made into an effective bonsai. The classic species grown as bonsai in Japan are: A. *buergerianum* and A. *palmatum*, the Japanese maple, and its cultivars, particularly 'Deshôjô', 'Kagiri-nishiki', 'Kashima', 'Katsura' and 'Seigen'.

PESTS

Other than the normal range of insects often found on any cultivated plants, maples are not often subject to serious insect infestations. The genus does not suffer from any specific insects or major predators, like elms (*Ulmus*), for example, suffer from Dutch elm disease. However, there are a number of problems that can occur.

Aphids

Aphids can be a problem in spring and early summer, causing damage to soft young growth and marking the foliage. Overwintering aphids emerge and increase rapidly. If left uncontrolled, they can stunt growth, as well as cause mis-shaped leaves. Proprietary pesticides used on a regular basis for two or three weeks will control the problem. They fall into three main catergories: winter washes, non-systemic contact insecticides and systemic insecticides. Winter washes are based on tar oil and are only used on fully dormant, deciduous woody plants. Non-systemic contact insecticides are mostly formulated as water-based sprays or as aerosols. Non-persistent formulations include derris, malathion, nicotine, pyrethrum and the newer synthetic pyrethroides – bio-resmethrin, permethrin and resmethrin. More persistent insecticides, which give longer protection, contain chemicals such as diazinon, fenitrothion, pirimicarb and pirimiphos-methyl. Systemic insecticides include dimethoate, formothion and menazon.

Scale

Maples, including Japanese maples, can be subject to attacks by a variety of scale insects. Recently, the hydrangea scale has become prevalent. In spring, small insects surrounded by a white wool may be seen on the underside of leaves. These pests feed on the plant's sap and excrete a honey dew, which makes the leaves of the plant sticky and encourages the growth of sooty moulds. The insects that you see are females. They can lay hundreds of eggs under waxy scales and their young, known as nymphs or crawlers, hatch some weeks later and disperse over plants before settling to feed, when they can cause a lot of damage.

I believe that the best line of defence is a winter wash with tar oil. Later in the year, control can be achieved by physically removing and killing the insects. To prevent build up of the problem, there should be a regular programme of spraying with non-persistent contact pesticides (see aphids, opposite). Timing is critical: the insecticide should be applied before the young crawlers have settled and started to form their protective scale – this is mainly in late spring and early summer.

Mites

Occasionally, infestations of spider mites, usually red spider mites, can occur, particularly when soil conditions are dry or plants are being grown under glass or in a polytunnel where the air is dry. A severe infestation is recognized by the top surface of the leaves becoming blotchy and paler in colour. When the leaf is turned over, the lower surface is found to be covered with colonies of very tiny red spider mites. A regular programme of spraying with an appropriate insecticide, such as derris, dicofol, malathion, dimethoate, formothion or diazinon, is necessary for control. A biological control *Phytoseiulus persimilis*, which preys on the mite, is available. Keeping the atmosphere damper with regular misting will help to prevent the recurrence of red spider mite.

Leaf miners

Leaf miners are caterpillars which overwinter in cocoons. In spring the females lay batches of eggs on the undersides of young leaves. The larvae hatch out about a week later and feed inside the leaves, making blister mines. When they have finished feeding, they come out of the mines, roll and tie the leaves with silk threads and then continue to feed within the protection of the rolled leaves.

Plants should be examined regularly and the caterpillars crushed when they are seen. The affected leaves can be removed and destroyed. Contact insectides (see aphids, opposite) are widely used. They include derris, bio-resmethrin and malathion; for longer-lasting control use permethrin or trichlorphon. In order to ensure effective control, soft soap should be added to the insecticide as a wetting agent.

Vine weevils

Vine weevils are a considerable pest and cause a great deal of damage. Fortunately, mature trees are not often endangered by vine weevil. It is young plants that are being grown in containers and seed trays that are most susceptible.

A. buergerianum has distinctive three-lobed leaves that turn scarlet and yellow in autumn.

Adult weevils lay their eggs during the late summer and early autumn. Upon hatching, the larvae enter the soil and start feeding on the roots. In mild climates, they will feed throughout the winter months and by spring only the woody portions of the root remain, and even these will be totally stripped of their cambium layers. The damage can be very extensive and a bad infestation will lead to many plants being lost.

The larvae are like small, white caterpillars. If they are detected in the soil, the plant should be taken out of the container and thorougly washed in a proprietary solution like Jeyes fluid. It can then be replanted in fresh soil.

Adult vine weevils are seldom seen as they are mainly nocturnal, hiding at soil level during the day and crawling up onto the plants after dark. Their presence is generally indicated by regular notches or holes eaten out of leaves.

Control of vine weevils is difficult. Any weevil or larvae that are seen should be destroyed immediately. There is a nematode biological control but, unfortunately, most of the available chemical treatments are not completely effective, although the recently introduced imidacloprid can keep the pest numbers down. Cleanliness is also important.

Mice, rabbits and squirrels

Mice can be an absolute pest as they will eat the seed and hide among the pots where they nibble at the young stems of plants. Maples with a sugary sap, like *A. saccharum*, are particular favourites. Mice can be controlled by putting down the pesticide Warfarin or by using traps.

Rabbits destroy top growth and also they can nibble at the bark of young trees. Plants can be protected by putting them in tubes, although these can be rather unsightly and obtrusive.

Squirrels are another pest which can cause enormous damage to young trees, stripping off the bark and exposing the cambium. While trees can recover from some attacks, it does cause damage which cannot always be repaired.

A mature specimen of *A. cissifolium* at Westonbirt Arboretum in Gloucestershire in winter.

Slugs and snails

Slugs and snails generally cause trouble during mild winters and in early spring. They are not much of a problem to established plants but they can cause a lot of damage to young seedlings by eating young growth. They can be combated by careful use of slug pellets or by using nematodes, which are watered into the soil. Other slug controls include inverted grapefruit or orange skins and beer traps.

DISEASES

One of the most common problems I have experienced, is the dying back of young twigs. It is often difficult to diagnose the cause of the problem as it can be a result of several organisms individually or in combination.

Verticillium

One of the main causes of dieback is verticillium wilt. Not only are young maples affected but also established plants. It is an ever-present threat in both gardens and larger landscapes.

Verticillium, itself, is a fungus. The damage it causes is thought to result from the blockage of the water-conducting tissues of the stem, so starving the leaves of water. It is now also believed that toxic substances may be produced by the fungus within the tissues. The death of the plant occurs quite quickly. With established plants, first one branch begins to die then another, until the whole plant is dead.

Verticillium wilt is very difficult to tackle satisfactorily. It is not fully understood how soil can get contaminated by the fungus or the exact stage of infection. Also, as yet there is no dependable cure.

As the fungus can lie in the soil for some time, it is better not to replant the infected area. Removing the contaminated soil is a possibility. This can be a difficult task as one can never be sure that one has cleaned out all infected areas and then it has to be replaced with good-quality clean soil.

It may be worthwhile trying a proprietary fungicide, such as benomyl or thiophanate-methyl, drenching the soil at regular intervals.

Fusarium

This is another fungus that may cause dieback or loss of young plants. The disease affects young seedlings as well as older plants. Control should be by a proprietary fungicide (see verticillium).

Acer tar spot (*Rhytisma acerinum*)

The sycamore, *A. pseudoplatanus*, is very prone to attack from tar spot fungus, which causes black bituminous blotches with yellow haloes. The fungus, which is unsightly but does not damage the trees, can also occur on other maples. Bordeaux mixture, sprayed regularly, can help, but on a large tree this is not feasible. Any affected fallen leaves should be collected and burnt.

Outbreaks of tar spot are less severe in industrial areas, where sulphur in the atmosphere may limit fungal development.

Botrytis

The fungus *Botrytis* is also a serious threat. It can cause the loss of young seedlings or instigate dieback in more established plants. The danger increases in warm, humid conditions, where there is insufficient air circulation. Control is achieved by the use of a proprietary fungicide such as Cheshunt Compound. It is possible to prevent damping off in young plants by watering emerging seedlings with Cheshunt Compound.

Coral spot (*Nectria cinnabarina*)

The symptoms of coral spot are masses of pinhead-size vivid coral pustules on dead and dying branches. It can occur as a saprophyte on dead branches or as a parasite on living branches causing dieback. Eradication is difficult. The diseased wood should be cut out and burnt, and the cuts treated with a wound sealant containing fungicide. The healthy parts of the plant should be sprayed immediately with a fungicide, such as thiophanate-methyl, and twice more at three-week intervals.

Scorch and twig burn

While not strictly a disease, leaf scorch and twig burn is a frequent problem. Twig burn can be caused by exposure to salt-laden winds, late spring frosts or exposure to hot sun. Leaf scorch can also occur if plants are watered on a hot sunny day, or as the result of irregular irrigation. Red-leaved maples, such as the cultivars of *A. palmatum*, such as 'Crimson Queen', are particularly prone to damage. Once damage occurs it is not treatable, so it is best to avoid it by protecting the trees from strong winds and frosts, and by watering regularly, and only in the evening during sunny weather.

Dieback

Young maples are particularly vulnerable to dieback. This is probably caused by the plant growing on late into the autumn so that the new wood does not harden before the onset of winter. The only treatment is to prune out any dead wood in the spring.

Chlorosis

Chlorosis is a disorder in which the leaves of the plant gradually turn yellow. It usually occurs if the maple is not properly cared for and may be the result of the soil being too alkaline (for an acid-loving plant), too wet (so that the roots cannot function properly) or due to a lack of iron.

Chlorosis is often also caused by a deficiency in magnesium, in which case an application of Epsom Salts will help. However, it can also be due to other mineral deficiencies, such as manganese, which can be corrected by spraying with manganese sulphate.

Once the leaves have turned yellow due to chlorosis, they will ususally remain that way until new ones grow the following year. However, if the chlorosis is caused by a deficiency, it is possible to defoliate the plant after the deficiency has been rectified. New leaves will grow in about two weeks and should be normal. This procedure should only be carried out once in any growing season.

Spring frosts

Unfortunately, now, possibly due to the much-publicized global warming, late spring frosts are becoming a serious problem. Often there is mild or warm weather in February or March which encourages the plants to come into growth. Then during April or early May there may be a severe frost that burns the soft young leaves and causes serious damage, perhaps even the death of the plant. Japanese maples are particularly susceptible. If a frost is forecast, then the plant should be protected by covering it with a net curtain or horticultural fleece. Young container-grown plants can be brought inside.

7
PROPAGATION

Maples may be propagated by seed, cuttings, grafting, budding or layering. They hybridize freely, so it is better to collect seed from an isolated tree or to use vegetative propagation, if you want to reproduce it exactly. An example is the Japanese maple (*A. palmatum*). A handful of seed collected from one plant and sown will produce seedlings that bear little or no resemblance to the mother plant, perhaps having a motley array of colour and leaf shapes.

One or two maples, for example *A. henryi*, can only be propagated by cuttings because they do not produce viable seed. *A. henryi* is dioecious (the male and female flowers are produced on separate trees) and, in Britain at least, only female forms are known. As no male trees have been found, any seed produced by the tree is not viable (parthenocarpic). At present, this maple has to be propagated by cuttings as there is no known understock onto which it can be successfully grafted.

A. diabolicum is also dioecious. No doubt in its native Japan, plants produce enough good fruits to survive, but it is very difficult to obtain seed from that country. Male and female plants do grow together in America, so seed sometimes becomes available, but it is very rare that both sexes are cultivated in Britain, so any seed produced in this country is usually parthenocarpic.

Maples may also be andromonoecious (the male and female flowers are on the same tree) and then fertilization usually occurs, resulting in a crop of good fruit. The seed can be tested by carefully cutting it open to see if there is an embryo inside. However, *A. griseum*, a highly desirable maple that is andromonoecious, is difficult to propagate as it produces abundant parthenocarpic fruits and few viable ones. This is because the flowers are produced separately. Thus, if the circumstances are not right because the pistils are not receptive or the stamens are not full of pollen, the female flowers will not be properly fertilized.

Seed-grown plants usually grow away well and easily. If the plants have hybridized with other species, the seedlings will easily be spotted as they grow much more quickly. Also, in some hybrid groups the seedlings will vary from the parent quite noticeably. For example, in the *A. opalus* group, the winter bud is mottled dark brown and green, whereas a true species has only a dark brown bud.

Cuttings may be more attractive to propagators than growing plants from seed as then you are truly reproducing the mother plant. This is very important in plants such as the Japanese maples, seed of which will not produce identical offspring.

Grafting is often preferred to cuttings as the plants grow away better and establish themselves more quickly. Also, it is not unknown for maples that are propagated by cuttings to collapse and die after four or five years. It is not clear what causes this phenomenon and, as far as I know, no research has been done so far.

Another method of propagation, budding, has a great advantage over grafting in that a parent tree will provide more buds for budding than scions for grafting, and the operation can be carried out in the summer.

SEED

The seed (samara) is a distinctive feature of the maple. There are usually two, sometimes three, seeds and these are joined at the head and each has a wing (see

A. palmatum 'Lutescens', its leaves turning rich yellow-gold in autumn, is propagated by cuttings or grafting.

p.16). The seeds are described as indehiscent as they do not break open when ripe, but are carried by the wind until they fall to the ground, from where they can be gathered. When ripe, the seed should no longer be green, but should be brown or may be some other colour, such as pink.

Seed of A. *rubrum* and A. *pycnanthum* ripens in early summer but all other seed ripens in the autumn. If it is to be collected from a private garden or park, permission should be sought from the owner. If seed is collected in the wild, then permission must be obtained from the appropriate authority and the provisions of the Convention on Biological Diversity (Rio de Janeiro 1992) complied with.

As soon as the seed is collected, it should be sown. It is not necessary to remove the seed wings, even though this is sometimes done. Maple seed is albuminous, the embryo being surrounded by a fluid that contains gibberellin acid – a growth hormone that acts as a food store for the little plant. The seed should never be laid out to dry as this will destroy the food store. Maple seed can be stored but then the moisture content should be reduced, slowly and carefully, to no less than about 20 degrees relative humidity. Then, when the seed is taken out for sowing, it should be soaked for 24 hours to re-introduce the moisture content.

Germination

The germination of a seed is not a mystery, but the work, or miracle, of nature. Taking the example of the sycamore (A. *pseudoplatanus*): the seed falls to the ground in the autumn, it is covered by the leaves as they fall, and in the spring it germinates. This tells us all we need to know about getting the seed to grow. When it falls, it is not ready to germinate and grow. What would be the point if the little tree started to grow in the autumn? It would get killed by the frost. It is better, therefore, to wait until the days lengthen and the weather is warmer. As it lies on the ground through the winter, the seed is exposed to all weathers, warmth, frost and rain. So here are two more ingredients to successful germination: moisture and fluctuating temperature. The seed, which is a living organism, needs these ingredients to stay alive through the winter, together

A. *shirasawanum* 'Aureum' has yellow leaves in spring which become darker in summer and turn to red in autumn.

COMPATIBLE MAPLES FOR GRAFTING

A. buergerianum is compatible with A. *paxii*.

A. davidii – All maples in Section Macrantha (see p.47) can be grafted onto A. *davidii*: A. *capillipes*, A. *crataegifolium*, also A. *crataegifolium* 'Veitchii', A. *forestii*, A. *kawakamii*, A. *micranthum*, A. *morifolium*, A. *pectinatum*, A. *pensylvanicum*, A. *taronense*.

A. griseum, A. *manchuricum*, A. *maximowiczianum* and A. *triflorum* are all compatible.

A. negundo – All cultivars of A. *negundo* can be grafted onto A. *negundo*.

A. palmatum – Japanese maple cultivars are usually grafted onto other Japanese maples.

All maples in Section Palmata (see p.46) can be grafted onto A. *palmatum*: A. *calcaratum*, A. *campbelli*, A. *circinatum*, A. *elegantulum*, A. *erianthum*, A. *flabellatum*, A. *laevigatum*, A. *oliverianum*, A. *robustum*, A. *shirasawanum*, A. *sieboldianum*, A. *takesimense*, A. *wilsoni*.

A. pentaphyllum can be grafted onto A. *pseudoplatanus* and sometimes also A. *saccharum*.

A. platanoides is a suitable understock for all in its section (Platanoidea, see p.50) except A. *campestre*. Thus it is compatible with A. *amplum*, A. *cappadocicum*, A. *cappadocicum* subsp. *sinicum*, A. *lobelli*, A. *mono*, A. *tenellum*, A. *truncatum* and A. *turkestanicum*. The grafting of A. *miyabei* is not very satisfactory as the plants are inclined to break away after a year or two.

A. pseudoplatanus – A. *caesium*, A. *giraldi*, A. *hyrcanum*, including its subspecies and cultivars, A. *monspessulanum*, including subspecies and cultivars, A. *obtusifolium*, A. *opalus* and A. *velutinum* can all be grafted onto A. *pseudoplatanus*.

A. *argutum* and A. *barbinerve* can be grafted onto A. *pseudoplatanus*, but this is not always successful and it produces many suckers.

A. *diabolicum* can sometimes be grafted onto A. *pseudoplatanus* but the plants are often very poor. The same problem arises with A. *franchetti*, A. *sino-purpurascens* and A. *villosum*. It is better to try two of the same group: for example, A. *villosum* and A. *franchetti*, or A. *sino-purpurascens* and A. *villosum* (see also A. *rubrum*, below).

A. rubrum is compatible with all its forms and clones as well as with A. *pycnanthum*. It may be possible to graft A. *franchetti*, A. *sino-purpurascens* and A. *villosum* onto A. *rubrum*, but a little more research needs to be done on this.

A. saccharum is compatible with all its subspecies and varieties.

A. spicatum – A. *ukurunduense* can be grafted onto A. *spicatum*.

A. tataricum can be used for its cultivars, for example 'Durand's Dwarf'.

---

with the food store in the nut. The lengthening days of spring and the stronger light and warmer days trigger the growth mechanism in the embryo.

In order to get seeds to germinate successfully in cultivation, we need to provide conditions that are similar to those it experiences in nature. The seed may be sown in pots or boxes between layers of sand in the autumn. Then, in spring, it can be washed out and sown in compost. Or, it can be sown in seed trays or in an open seed bed, also in the autumn. The seed must be protected against vermin and, if it is outside, it must not be allowed to get too wet, otherwise it may rot.

Another, and perhaps better method is to put the seed, mixed with a little damp, not wet, peat into a polythene bag, sealing it and then placing it in a secure box, which is then put in a box in an unheated garden shed, so it is safe from mice and other vermin. The seed should be examined every week to see if germination has started. If a little white root is coming out of the nutlet, then the seed may be sown in a good compost. Some seeds germinate in the first spring after collection, but those that have a hard woody coat (for example A. *griseum* and A. *triflorum*) do not germinate for two years. Seed of A. *campestre* collected green in early autumn often germinates more quickly in the following spring but seed that is collected late may not germinate for two years.

Seed may also be put in the refrigerator before

sowing to expose it to the correct conditions. Good results can be achieved, so long as one or two points are borne in mind: it is important to keep check on how moist the seed is as the cold air inside a refrigerator is dry; and it is difficult to be definitive on how long the seed should be kept in the refrigerator – some seeds (for example, *A. truncatum*) can germinate quickly, but others (see above) may take longer to germinate. It is often suggested that seed should be placed in the refrigerator for a short time, then taken out for another period and then put back in for another period, before sowing. This idea seems to be borne out by the effects of the fluctuating temperatures that the seeds would experience in the wild.

CUTTINGS

Many maples can be propagated by cuttings. Those taken from juvenile plants root much more easily than those taken from mature plants so it is a good idea to bring stock plants into the greenhouse early in the year to force them into growth. Cuttings of the new shoots can then be taken in early spring. This method is not the easiest for amateurs. Cuttings from open-ground plants are normally taken in early summer, when the young shoots start to harden, but before they mature. Hardwood cuttings may be taken in late summer but are not always successful (see below).

Take a cutting by removing the shoot just below a bud. Then remove the lower leaves and reduce the size of other leaves so as to minimize the loss of water through transpiration.

Rooting is encouraged if a growth hormone is used. Indolybuturic acid is probably the most satisfactory with a concentration of about 0.8%, although up to 2% appears to be safe. It is available in both powdered and liquid form. The base of the cutting is dipped into it before being inserted into compost.

Rooting the cuttings

Although a number of different compost mixes may be used to root the cuttings, an equal mixture of peat and sand is quite adequate. Once the cuttings are inserted in the medium, put them under polythene, or if you have the facilities, constant or intermittent misting. If polythene is used, adequate shading, particularly in the summer, must be given to prevent the cuttings being burnt.

The next stage, the establishment of the rooted cuttings, is often problematic because they are so vulnerable to damage. They need to be weaned from the protected environment that they are in. This must be done gradually to give them the time to adjust to normal conditions. If the cuttings have been rooted under polythene, this can be lifted a little each day to allow more and more air in; if they are under a mister, the misting can be reduced slowly. Once the cuttings have been fully weaned, they can be placed in pots making sure that the roots are disturbed as little as possible.

It is important to try to get the rooted cuttings into growth before the onset of winter. This is the reason why it is better to take them as early in the year as possible. Losses incurred during the winter can usually be traced to the fact that the rooted cuttings have not established a good root system and that there has not been sufficient regrowth. Also, it is suggested that rooted cuttings, like seed (see above), may need a cold period in winter. A common practice is to put the young cuttings in a cold frame over the winter so that they experience cold but are not exposed to frost.

Hardwood cuttings of maples have not proved satisfactory. If this method is to be tried then the cuttings should be 20–22cm (8–9in) long. They will root better if they are wounded, which involves removing a piece of bark about 1cm (½in) long from the base of the cutting to expose the cambium. They should then be plunged into a bed of sand, or sand and peat, with about 7cm (3in) of the cutting above ground.

GRAFTING

Grafting usually takes place either in the summer or in mid- to late winter. Many propagators prefer to graft the maple species in winter and Japanese maples in the summer. The preparation for grafting and aftercare requires a lot of attention. Hygiene is absolutely essential and the grafting knife must be sterilized at each stage.

Before the actual operation of grafting, the understocks, that is the plants onto which the piece (scion) of the mother plant is to be grafted, are brought into the greenhouse to be dried off and to reduce the flow of sap. This drying-off period is important because if scions are grafted onto a stock plant that is full of sap, the sap may flood the scion wood and kill it.

Scions are best taken in the early morning. They

PLATE VII

A selection of maple species and cultivars

A. *crataegifolium* 'Veitchii'

A. *japonicum* 'Aconitifolium'

A. *cissifolium*

All leaves are shown at approximately half lifesize

A. *pseudoplatanus* 'Simon-Louis Frères'

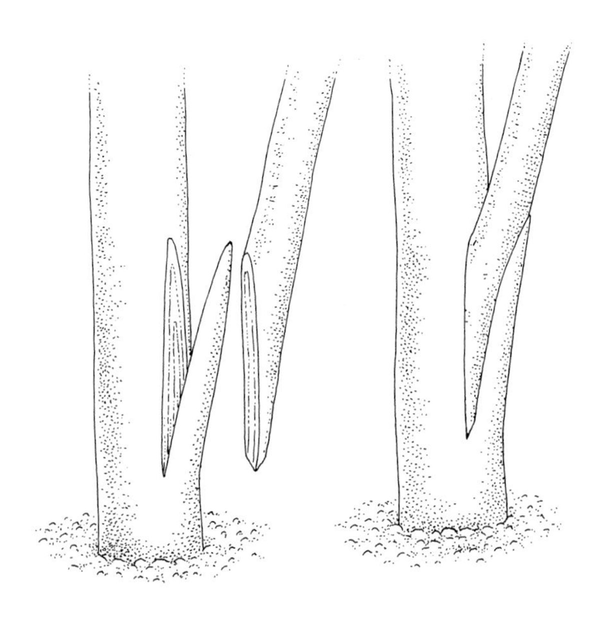

In a side veneer graft, the stock and scion are prepared (left) and then the scion is inserted (right).

should be of the current season's growth, about 15cm (6in) long and have 4 or 5 buds or leaves on them. The leaves are usually removed or the top half is cut off. It is important that the mother plants are free from disease, pests or viruses, and are in good condition. Scions can be taken of older growth but are sometimes slower to callus and, therefore, more vulnerable to failure.

Side veneer graft

There are several methods of grafting, but the one most often used is a side veneer graft.

With a side veneer graft, the scion need not have all its leaves removed. Once the scion material is obtained, it is cut at the base with an even spliced cut of about 2.5cm (1in) long. The stock plant is prepared by making a cut of the same length in the bark, making sure that the cambium is exposed, but not damaged: it is the cambium that plays the most important part in the success of the graft. The scion is then fitted into the cut and tied firmly in place with an elasticated rubber strip.

When the grafts are complete they should be placed in a frame with some bottom heat – an even temperature of 20°C (68°F) is required. The frame can either be on the floor or on a greenhouse bench, but it should have a glass or polythene top and wood or brick sides. The newly-grafted plants need humidity, so about 1cm (½in) of well-watered peat should be put on top of the soil-warming cables. The grafts are more likely to succeed if they are at an angle, so the pots should be tilted so that they are partially immersed in the peat.

The stock plant responds to the graft by producing new growth at the site of the wound. This growth, which protrudes slightly, is known as the callus. As soon as the union has callused, plants can be weaned in a similar way to cuttings. Air is allowed into the frame, a little more each day. After four or five weeks, when the union is strong enough and the scion has begun to grow, the plants can be watered. Then the top of the stock plant above the graft can be removed gradually.

Choosing understocks

Understocks must be in good condition and free from disease. In such a large family, with a considerable range and diversity of plants, it is not surprising that some incompatibility occurs between the various species and so specific understocks need to be chosen with care. For example, a maple with a milky sap, such as *A. platanoides*, cannot be grafted onto a maple that does not have milky sap, such as *A. saccharum*. It is suggested that maples in the same section (see p.134) are compatible. However, this is not always the case: *A. campestre* and *A. platanoides* both have a milky sap and are in the same section, but they are incompatible.

A. pseudoplatanus and *A. rubrum* have both proved to be understocks that are compatible with many maples, even those outside their own section. The list (p.134) shows which species are compatible.

BUDDING

Budding involves taking a bud or 'eye' attached to a portion of the bark and transferring it to another specimen of the same plant or to a different, but compatible plant (see list p.134). There are many ways of performing the operation but the principal method is called 'T-budding'.

Suitable healthy and disease-free root stocks are planted in late autumn for propagation the following year. The budding stock is budded when the sap is in free circulation as this is when the bark will detach itself easily from the wood on being gently lifted.

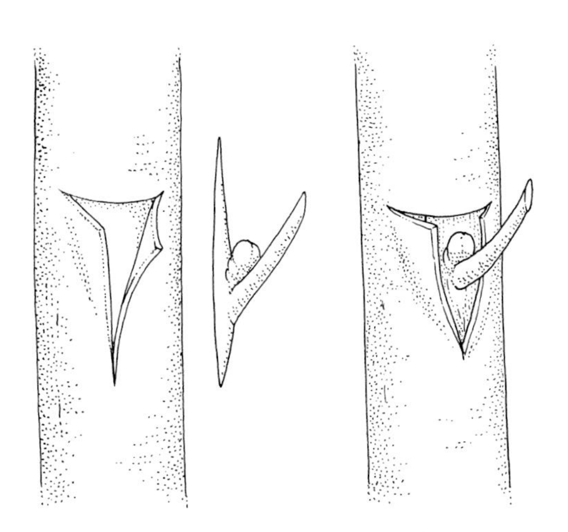

In a T-bud graft, a T shaped cut is made in the bark of the stock (left) into which a prepared bud is inserted (right).

The root stock is prepared first by removing any dead wood and ensuring that it is in good condition. Then, using a sterilized knife, a T-shaped incision is made in the bark, which is then lifted gently aside. It does not seem to be important where the incision is made, but it should be low down to ensure that the eventual plant is tidy in appearance.

The bud is prepared by inserting the knife about 1cm (½in) below it, then gradually sliding the blade upwards and inwards under the bud, before bringing it out by cutting through the bark at about 1cm (½in) above it. During the operation a piece of wood will also be sliced out and this can be removed from the bud and bark section. It is usually removed very gently, starting from the top of the bud section and peeling down to the bottom. At this stage, great care must be taken not to pull out the base, or root, of the bud as this would render it useless.

The bud is then fitted into the T-shaped incision in the stock plant, and is tied in place with a soft material, such as raffia, to prevent the entry of water and insects. The budded plant must now be shaded from the sun for a few days.

If budding is not successful, this may be because the delicate eye has been bruised, or there may be a virus present.

LAYERING

Maples can also be propagated by layering. In commercial practice stock plants, which are called stools, are cultivated to produce as many young shoots as possible. The shoots, or layer leads, are pegged down into the soil or into a pot filled with compost in the spring, after the bark has been 'nicked' so as to expose a little of the cambium and thus encourage rooting. It is easy to produce one or two layers from a home-grown plant. An even bud break (eg two buds opposite each other) should be encouraged from the young layers so that well-formed trees result. Layers should root in a year and be ready for lifting the following autumn.

In a layer, a branchlet close to the ground is prepared by nicking the bark and is then pegged into the soil.

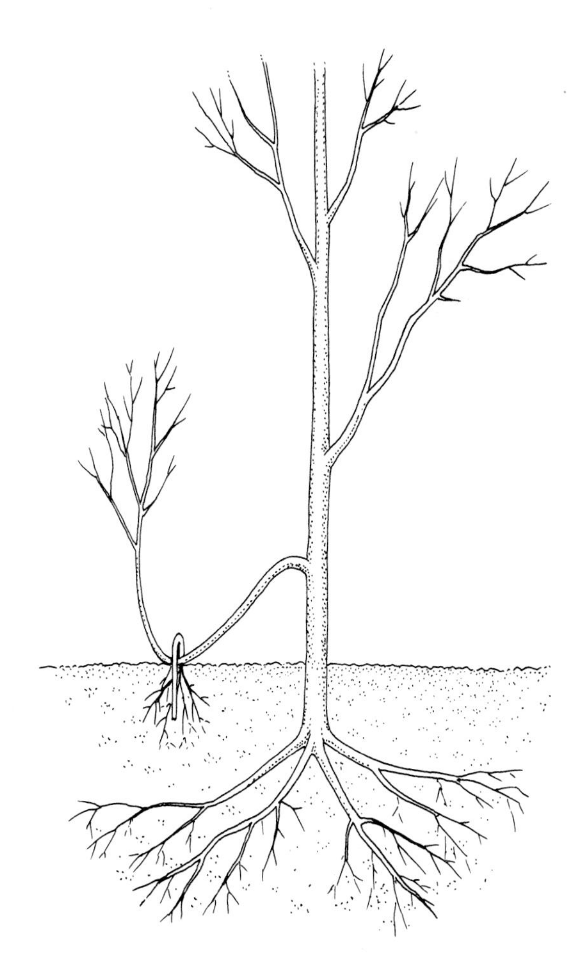

8

MAPLES IN THE GARDEN & LANDSCAPE

Maples are a dominant part of the landscape in many countries. Frederick Law Olmsted, the American landscape architect, wrote in 1893: "The root of all my good work is an early respect for, regard and enjoyment of scenery ... and extraordinary opportunities for cultivating susceptibility to the power of scenery." The "scenery" he was referring to was "not so much grand or sensational scenery, as scenery of a more domestic order. Scenery to be looked upon contemplatively and which is provocative of musing moods." Olmsted's love of nature was not "such as is shown in admiration of flowers in a vase, or even in admiration for a *hortus sciens* or a botanic garden", but rather love that led him to "take quiet drives upon meadow and woodland roads for the most part, regarding the scenery silently, and never in a way to lead to exclamations." Among the plants Olmsted would have witnessed on his travels in his native land are the maples, which are so common to the landscape of North America.

The experience of scenery is visual. Olmsted described it thus: "A man's eyes cannot be as much occupied as they are in large cities by artificial things ... without a harmful effect first on his mental and nervous system, and ultimately on his entire constitutional organisation." To him, scenery provided a relief and was able "to refresh and delight the eye, and through the eye, the mind and the spirit." The beautiful and varied colours of the maples and their myriad forms are capable of providing this refreshment and delight.

Autumn in the botanical gardens at Bath in Somerset with maples forming an important part of the colourful display.

It is a never-to-be-forgotten experience to travel through America and to witness the more intimate landscapes, as well as those that are sensational. Spring is an uplifting time, full of the soft greens of the maples and other trees with the woodland flowers underneath. In autumn, nature takes out her palette, painting the countryside with a rich array of colour. The beauty of the maples, oaks, birch and sweet gum growing along the riverbanks, their bright hues reflecting in the water, is breathtaking.

JAPAN

The Japanese have held a veneration for the natural world and a delight in its beauties for centuries. Japan's first holy places were natural features – a special rock or a water feature often adorned by a maple. It is because of the special relationship that the Japanese have with nature that, for them, plants symbolize certain spiritual qualities. Their gardens are often designed to represent the essential elements of earth, fire and water. Another theme that may be portrayed is the journey through life and even into death. The sequence of germination, growing and flowering leading to autumn, with its fruit and falling foliage, is a representation of man's destiny. The wind blowing the leaves away in autumn represents the passing of life.

The Japanese call the maple 'Momiji' and it is hardly possible to imagine a temple garden without at least one of these highly respected trees. The valley of the maples by Dragon Lake in the gardens of Shugako-in on the outskirts of Kyoto is a most beautiful sight and deserving of a visit. It contains varieties of Japanese maples with colourful azaleas along mossy banks and beside steps.

The garden contains three separate villas, linked by pine avenues and set against a forested background. From the upper villa, all Kyoto can be seen within its encirling bowl of hills. This garden, which is on a slope, contains many varieties of Japanese maples, as well as clipped evergreens and pines; it is a wonderful example of *shakkei* – a borrowed landscape.

As the year draws to a close, and autumn comes on, the spectacle of the Japanese countryside draws millions to it. Prominent in the autumn display are the maples, usually dressed in rich red but often with tones of yellow and gold. In Britain, likewise, tens of thousands of people are drawn to such spectacles as the *Acer* glade at Westonbirt Arboretum (see p.149).

MAPLES IN THE GARDEN

In our own gardening, it is not the wide, open vistas that concern us, but rather the small, intimate landscapes that can form a part of our own plot. The garden is an extra room to the house. It forms a green oasis where one can find peace – relief from the stress of daily life. Some people may wish to enjoy the garden by resting in it, others may find enjoyment in the activity of gardening. Indeed, the garden can satisfy many different tastes: it can be a place of beauty and quiet, or it can be a place of industry, where vegetables are grown.

Because of their diversity of form and colour, maples are ideal plants for gardens. Fortunately, through the efforts of plant hunters and explorers, we now have a vast reservoir of beautiful plants to choose for our gardens, among them many beautiful maples. It is possible to find maples that are suitable for every corner of the garden and, in addition, that are attractive and interesting all the year round.

Winter

The ideal garden needs to have something of interest in all four seasons – winter, spring, summer and autumn – with the winter being just as important as the summer. So, ideally, the plants chosen should have qualities that will make them attractive in all seasons. Maples fit this criterion particularly well. In winter their outline shape and form, with the tracery of their branches, is something of beauty. Add to this the

An impressive and attractive specimen of *A. palmatum* at Westonbirt Arboretum.

A. palmatum 'Dissectum Atropurpureum' belongs to the Dissectum Group, which has delicate filigreed foliage.

extraordinary barks that many species display (*A. griseum*, *A. truncatum* and the snake bark maples), and one has a wonderfully valuable winter asset. In fact, one could argue that the real qualities of these plants are hidden by the leaves during the summer. The bark of *A. griseum* or *A. triflorum* sparkling in the winter snow is awe inspiring. And the bark of the snake bark maples and the coral bark maple, *A. palmatum* 'Sango-kaku', is much more vivid in winter. The latter compares very favourably with the dogwoods (*Cornus*).

The buds and young stems of many maples are also a delight in winter, particularly on a crisp, sunny day. *A. capillipes* has beautiful purplish-red stems and buds. *A. acuminatum* and *A. barbinerve* have wonderful reddish young stems. Then there is *A. palmatum* 'Aoyagi', which has striking green stems.

Spring

At the beginning of the year, in spring, a new scene unfolds itself. Nature presents us with another rich tapestry of colour. At this time a maple variety with soft green leaves, such as *A. shirasawanum* 'Aureum' with its attractive lime-green foliage, delights the eye. Indeed, the range of greens seen in the springtime forests of which the maples are part, are too beautiful and varied to be described.

Aside from green, many maples have bronze or purple foliage, which is particularly eye-catching when it first unfurls. These include *A. truncatum*, *A. capillipes*, *A. nikoense* and some cultivars of *A. palmatum*. Many *A. palmatum* cultivars, especially the red-leafed varieties, have a wonderful array of bronze and reddish-purple young foliage in spring. *A. palmatum* 'Higasayama' is notable for its pale creamy-yellow unfolding leaves, contrasting with the long red sheaves. *A. palmatum* 'Beni-maiko' and *A. palmatum* 'Deshôjô', among others, have brilliant shrimp-pink young foliage. *A. palmatum* 'Katsura' has an orangey foliage that is truly breathtaking. *A. cappadocicum* 'Rubrum' has striking reddish foliage, while the leaves of *A. cappadocicum* 'Aureum' are a rich yellow.

At the same time, many maples are adorned with flowers. The yellow blossoms of *A. platanoides* opening just before the leaf buds break are a memorable sight. Other maples with notable flowers include *A. velutinum* (*A. insigni*) which has upright spikes, like candles on the tree, and *A. opalus*. Some maples have flowers with crimson or red tepals: these include *A. palmatum*, *A. japonicum* and *A. circinatum*, and are also most attractive. *A. rubrum* starts its annual display with long tassles of reddish flowers in mid-spring.

Summer

The summer is another season when maples can be appreciated for the diversity of their foliage. This ranges from the large, bold leaves of *A. villosum* and *A. macrophyllum*, to the small, neat leaves of *A. monspessulanum* and *A. buergerianum*. The leaves can be in leaflets, like those of *A. cissifolium*, or they can be entire, like those of *A. carpinifolium*. This is just one of the features that make the genus so marvellous for companion planting – there is always one that will be appropriate for the site. For delicate, filigreed foliage, choose the Japanese maple (*A. palmatum*) or select a specimen from the *A. palmatum* Dissectum Group, with their the lace-like leaves. For tiny leaves, *A. palmatum* 'Goshiki-kotohime' and *A. palmatum* 'Hanami-nishiki' are ideal, and they contrast well with the bolder leaves of *A. palmatum* 'Bloodgood' and *A. palmatum* 'Ôsakazuki'.

Autumn

The autumn is the final bouquet. Then the rich diversity of this family can really be appreciated, many leaves turning rich scarlet or yellow or gold. The spectacle in Japan has already been mentioned. In Korea the mountainsides are ablaze with the rich tints of the maples among other stunning autumn plants, such as euonymous, magnolia, birch, spice bush and many others. Each maple often gives an individual display. In America the widespread native maple *A. saccharum* usually turns yellow, although sometimes one can find trees that turn red, along with *A. rubrum*, making the American landscape come alive with colour. The North American Indians have a picturesque interpretation of what happens during this season: "The hunters of the Milky Way killed the Great Bear with a shooting star, his blood dripped on the trees below, the Great Bear was then cut up and cooked in the Big Dipper. The now-tired hunters slept and the fat from the boiling pot spilt on the remaining leaves, turning them to yellow and brown."

SIZE AND SHAPE

It need not be repeated that there are a vast number of possibilities for planting maples in the park or garden when size or shape is important.

The forest tree-like species, for example *A. pseudoplatanus*, *A. platanoides*, *A. macrophyllum* and *A. cappadocicum*, are superb park specimens. Each makes a round-headed tree and, seen from a distance, they all have an attractive form and shape. *A. cappadocicum* has the added bonus of its foliage turning yellow in autumn. *A. platanoides* can also turn a little yellow. These trees are good subjects for planting in large gardens, where they provide shade to sit under and to shelter other plants.

A medium-sized garden requires trees that do not become too dominant. *A. capillipes* can make the most beautiful specimen. Growing to about 11m (35ft), it matures to a round-headed tree and does need some space. If a place can be found for it, then it will bring interest and character. It has attractive foliage that turns scarlet in autumn, and in winter it displays its beautiful snake bark, which is purplish-red with white striations, later becoming greenish or greyish-green.

Smaller, and very neat in habit, is *A. rufinerve* from Japan, which makes an upright tree. Its foliage turns scarlet in autumn and in winter it shows off its snake bark, which is green with white striations. *A. griseum* is an absolute gem that can be planted on its own or in a group. Its handsome leaves consist of three leaflets and turn scarlet in autumn, but its chief attraction is its wonderful cinnamon-coloured bark. It has deservedly been awarded the Award of Garden Merit by the Royal Horticultural Society and it is a tree that will grow in all soils, so long as they are not wet. It grows slowly, making an upright tree with an open crown.

Shrubby maples

A. palmatum, *A. japonicum* and *A. circinatum* are shrubby maples that are wonderful subjects for planting in a border or with other trees. The foliage will contrast well with other plants, and towards the end of the year one has the beauty of their rich autumn tints. Their effect will be enhanced if they are placed against a dark background to mimic the edge of the forest where they are so often found growing in their native country.

These maples also grow well in semi-shade, so if there are some mature trees in the garden, they can be planted in between. The early morning and evening light enhances the foliage in such positions. As these species prefer a deep, moist, well-drained soil, they should not be planted too close to the taller trees, which will be making the soil dry as they take up moisture for themselves.

A. *truncatum* with its attractive roughish bark is wide-spreading in growth and its glossy green foliage turns scarlet in autumn. A. *buergerianum* is more upright. It also has glossy green leaves in summer; these turn from yellow to scarlet before falling.

When choosing for shape, one must always consider A. *palmatum* and its cultivars. They can either be planted in conjunction with other trees and shrubs or in groups on their own, where they will create a rich tableau in a variety of foliage textures and colours. These are graceful plants that are very adaptable as they will grow in most soil – alkaline as well as acid, so long as it is well-drained, as they do not like their feet in water. Many of the cultivars grow satisfactorily in full sun. Easy to grow, they are wonderful plants that give satisfaction and pleasure for many years.

The mounds of lace-like foliage of A. *palmatum* 'Dissectum' cascading over the edge of a pond and reflecting in the water is a joyful sight. Just as effective a use of this lovely maple can be made in the rock garden or as a single specimen. Its leaves can be green or purplish-red in the summer.

Rock gardens and containers

A rock garden can be enhanced by a Japanese maple. Two dwarf cultivars are ideal and make a marvellous foil for other plants. They are A. *palmatum* 'Little Princess', which grows to about 60cm (2ft) high and spreads to about 90cm (3ft), and A. *palmatum* 'Kotohime', which also grows to about 60cm (2ft) and is more upright in habit.

Japanese maples have fibrous roots and so they are also ideally suited for growing in containers, which can then be placed around the garden or on the patio. Patios often attract heat in the summer, so if the maple is placed there, it may need a little protection especially if the foliage is variegated or delicate. Growing a maple in a container enables one to get greater pleasure as it can be moved around the garden to different positions through the seasons. Make sure you choose an attractive pot and then you can use the plant and pot to complement a feature in the garden like, for example, a seat or a small statue. Place a potted maple at the end of a path against a dark background and you will have a wonderful effect.

Variegated maples

The variegated maples are sometimes difficult to place in gardens, even though they are very beautiful. As Olmsted commented, "the unconscious operation of nature's restorative power is hindered by specimen planting, spots of brightly coloured flowers or any use of a plant that calls attention to itself". Thus, the placing in the garden of variegated maples needs careful thought.

A. *palmatum* 'Butterfly' is a most charming plant. Its matt-green foliage is mottled with cream markings and it has an upright habit. Though it makes a splendid specimen tree, it may be more difficult to place in the midst of a mixed planting of trees and shrubs. A. *negundo* 'Flamingo' is a popular and striking maple whose young foliage is a bright pink and green, sometimes with some white. It is best cut back in late winter or early spring each year to encourage young growth and brighter foliage. This is another example of a plant that is attractive as an isolated specimen but difficult to grow in a mixed planting of other trees and shrubs.

Coping with dry spots

In drier parts of the garden, maples such as A. *monspessulanum* and A. *ginnala* will thrive. A. *monspessulanum* comes from southern Europe and so is adapted to dry summer conditions. The natural habitat of A. *ginnala* stretches from Turkestan in the west to China in the east. It is a most accommodating maple, being able to grow on dry, poor soil, yet giving a wonderful autumn display, with attractive fruits with red wings. It also complements other trees and shrubs in mixed plantings.

Hedges

A. *ginnala* can also be used as a hedge. More commonly used is the field maple (A. *campestre*), which has

An A. *palmatum* cultivar in full summer leaf at Tatton Park in Cheshire.

A. *ginnala* has beautiful autumn colours and makes a very effective hedge.

attractive pinkish young foliage, and turns yellow or scarlet in autumn. It is ideal for hedging as it can stand regular cutting. One of the best hedges of field maples I have seen is in the garden of J. D Vertrees in Oregon. Many other species have been tried as hedges, including A. *buergerianum* and A. *monspessulanum*, both of which can stand regular cutting. A. *monspessulanum*, in particular, is used as hedging in France and elsewhere.

Urban landscaping

The choice of trees for urban landscapes is limited as trees planted here have to endure pollution and often restricted sites. All too frequently, the soil gets compacted and then the air that is essential for growth cannot reach the roots in sufficient quantities to keep the tree healthy. A. *pseudoplatanus* and A. *platanoides* can withstand such conditions. However, A. *pseudoplatanus* has one problem. It has thick, leathery leaves that do not break down easily after they fall in autumn – these can make the pavements slippery.

More useful are some of the cultivars of these maples. On pavements, which are not always very wide, one does not want to have a wide-spreading tree: A. *platanoides* 'Globosum' is ideal for such a site as it makes a small, round-headed tree, and it grows well in urban areas. The London plane, *Platanus × hispanica* is often chosen for city planting as it can be pollarded. Maples do not take kindly to pollarding, so it is better to use an upright form, which will not need trimming – for example the strong-growing A. *platanoides* 'Columnare'.

In the parks in towns and cities, people want to wander or sit and enjoy the plants in peace and quiet. For such situations a wider range of maples can be selected. They will not suffer from the same compacting of soil that occurs around pavements, although if the air is polluted then some may not thrive well. It is important to choose some that will grow into trees as these will be appreciated for their shade and impact. Suitable species include A. *platanoides*, A. *trautvetteri*, A. *capillipes*, A. *cappadocidum* and A. *cappadocicum* 'Aureum', A. *griseum*, although this is slow-growing, and A. *saccharum* and A. *mono*.

MAPLE COLLECTIONS

The botanic gardens at Kew and Edinburgh, those of the Natural History Museum in Paris and the Natural History Museum in Vienna, as well as those at Dahlem and the Spath Arboretum in Berlin, the Arnold Arboretum in Boston and the National Arboretum in Washington are just some of the places where great collections of maples can be enjoyed. The plants in these garden have been gathered from all over the world. Many of the original plants collected by the great plant hunters, such as Wilson and Forrest, are still growing in places such as Kew.

In the 1820s Mr Holford, with remarkable skill and foresight, planned and laid out an extensive arboretum at Westonbirt in Gloucestershire. Today, these trees have reached maturity and people flock to Westonbirt in the autumn to enjoy the maples' full autumn magnificence, and the gardens and woods are brilliant with crimson, scarlet and gold. Maples at Westonbirt include a wide range of Japanese maples: in the *Acer* glade, they are specially selected forms grown from seed, not named cultivars; the Silk Wood contains a good collection of named cultivars. Other maples that add to the autumnal display include A. *cappadocicum*, A. *carpinifolium*, A. *griseum*, A. *henryi*, A. *nikoense*, A. *rubrum* and A. *saccharum*.

Such wonderful scenes can also be enjoyed at Wakehurst in Kent, which is part of the Royal Botanic Gardens, at Savill Gardens in Windsor Great Park, and at many National Trust gardens, of which perhaps the most striking is Sheffield Park in East Sussex. The Sir Harold Hillier Gardens and Arboretum near Romsey in Hampshire is also renowned for its collection of maples as well as many other trees and shrubs, all growing in a beautiful landscape.

Many other European countries have wonderful old parks. These include the Gimborne Arboretum and the Trompenburg Arboretum in Holland, Wilhelmshohe and Karlsaue in Kassel in Germany, the Forest Garden of Tharandt in East Germany, Pruhonice in Czechoslovakia and Kalmthout in Belgium, to mention a few.

In America, the Arnold Arboretum near Boston, which was founded in 1872 with Charles Sprague Sargent as director, has a wide variety of interesting plants. Sargent was determined to make it into an internationally renowned arboretum. It has participated in many plant-hunting expeditions and contains many of the original plants collected.

A. *cappadocicum* is an adaptable species that is suitable for urban landscaping.

The University of Washington Arboretum in Seattle has a fine collection of maples, established by the former director B. O. Mulligan. The arboretum also contains an attractive Japanese garden.

Other excellent collections of maples are to be found at the United States National Arboretum in Washington DC, the Morton Arboretum in Illinois and the Morris Arboretum in Philadelphia, which has some outstanding specimens of such species as A. *buergerianum*.

APPENDICES

APPENDIX 1
GLOSSARY

Acuminate Having a gradually diminishing point.
Andromonoecious A plant that has perfect flowers (that is male and female flowers together) and male flowers individually, but no female flowers.
Attenuate Narrowed or tapered.
Calyx The outer covering or leaf-like envelope of a flower.
Clone Any group of plants propagated from a single mother plant and reproduced vegetatively.
Cordate Heart-shaped.
Corymb A flat-topped or open flower cluster.
Crenate Scalloped. (Crena is a rounded tooth or notch.)
Cultivar A horticultural or garden variety created by human activity.
Cyme A broad or flattened flower cluster. (Note: in a racemose inflorescence, the end of the axis does not produce a flower but goes on growing, the flowers being borne on lateral branches. In a cymose inflorescence, the growth of the axis is limited by the formation of a terminal flower.)
Dioecious A plant that has male and female flowers on different trees.
Entire Without toothing or division, with an even margin – in leaves, for example.
Glabrous Smooth, without hairs.
Glaucous Covered with a bloom, as in a plum.
Internode Between the nodes, that is between where the leaves or the buds are.
Lanceolate Narrow, tapering to each end.
Lenticels Corky spots on young bark.
Lobe A division of the leaf.
Marcescent Leaves that wither and do not fall off.

The wild garden at Pyrford Court Gardens in Surrey, with young and old Japanese maples providing colour.

Monoecious A plant that has male and female flowers on the same tree.
Node The part of a stem or branch that normally has a leaf.
Oblong Much longer than broad, with nearly parallel sides.
Obtuse Blunt or rounded at the end.
Ovate Shaped like a longitudinal section of a hen's egg, the broader end at the base.
Panicle A loose flower cluster.
Parthenocarpic The production of fruit without true fertilization, such fruit have no embryos and cannot grow.
Raceme Flowers with a lengthened axis, like a bunch of grapes.
Reticulate Netted. For example, a network of veins.
Rugose Covered with wrinkles.
Samara A winged fruit that remains closed at maturity and does not break open.
Scale Any thin, dry, not green body. For example, scaly bark is bark that peels off in scale-like portions, such as that of sycamore.
Sepals The individual segments of a calyx.
Serrate With teeth on the margin that are directed towards the end of the leaf.
Serrulate Serrate but with very small teeth.
Sinus The recess or gap between the lobes of a leaf.
Species A collection of all those individuals that have the same constant and distinctive characters.
Truncate As though cut off at the end. A truncate leaf is cut straight at its end.
Type The ideal representative of the species.
Variety A plant that differs slightly but distinctly from the species to which it belongs, but not so much as to be a subspecies.
Villous Bearing long weak hairs.

APPENDIX 2
READING ABOUT MAPLES

A selection of books and journals in which more information about maples may be found.

Bean, W.J. *Trees and Shrubs Hardy in the British Isles – Volume 1*, (8th Edition, Murray, London, 1970).

Bean, W.J. *Trees and Shrubs Hardy in the British Isles – Supplement* (Murray, London, 1988).

Bretschneider, E. *History of European Botanical Discoveries in China* (Leipzig, 1898, reprint 1981).

Cowan, J.M. *The Journeys and Plant Introductions of George Forrest* (Oxford University Press, 1952).

Davis, P.H. *Flora of Turkey* (1965 *et seq.*).

Elwes, H.J. and Henry, A. *The Trees of Great Britain and Ireland* – Volume 3, pp.630–686 (Edinburgh 1906–13, republished by SR Publishers Ltd., 1969).

Evelyn, J. *Sylva* (London Council of the Royal Society, 1664).

Fang, W.P. *A Monograph of Chinese Aceraceae* (Contributions from the Biological Laboratory of the Science Society of China – Nanking, China, 1939).

Fang, W.P *Flora Reipublicae Popularis Sinicae* Volume 46 (1981).

Hardÿ de Beaulieu, A. *Guide Illustré des Erables* (1998).

Hosie, R.C. *Native Trees of Canada* (Fitzhenry and Whiteside Ltd, Ontario and Canadian Forestry Service, Canada, 8th edition 1979).

Koidzumi 'Revisio Aceracearum Japonicarum' *Journal of the College of Science* Imperial University of Tokyo, 1911.

Krussman, G. *Manual of Cultivated Broad Leaved Trees & Shrubs* (Timber Press, Oregon, 1984).

Kurata, S. *Illustrated Important Forest Trees of Japan* Volumes 1–5 (Tokyo, 1964–1976).

Lancaster, R. 'Maples of Himalayas', *Journals of the Royal Horticultural Society* Volume 101 p.589, 1976.

Li, H.L. *Woody Flora of Taiwan* (Livingston, Pennsylvania, 1963).

Maple Society *The International Register for Japanese Maples*.

Mitchell, A.F. *A Field Guide to the Trees of Great Britain and Northern Ireland* (Collins, London, 1974).

Mulligan, B.O. *Maples Cultivated in the United States and Canada* (American Association of Botanic Gardens and Arboreta, Pennsylvania, 1958).

Murray, K.E. *A Monograph of the Aceraceae* (Pennsylvania State University, 1970).

Nicholson, G. 'The Kew Arboretum, The Maples' I–XVI *Gardener's Chronicle* 1881, Volume 15, pp.10, 42, 74–75, 136, 137, 141, 172, 268, 299, 364, 499, 532, 564, 725, 788.

Nicholson, G. 'The Kew Arboretum, The Maples' I–XVI *Gardener's Chronicle* 1882, Volume 16, pp.75, 136, 375, 590, 719, 750, 815.

Pax, F. 'Aceraceae' in *Das Pflanzenreich* IV. 163 by A. Engler (1902).

Pirc, H. *Ahorne* (Eugen Ulmer GMßH, 1994).

Rehder, A. *Manual of Cultivated Trees & Shrubs* (Macmillan, New York, 1927).

Sargent, C.S. *Forest Flora of Japan* (Tokyo, 1894, reprint 1939).

Sargent, C.S. *Plantae Wilsonianae* Volume 1 (Arnold Arboretum, Boston, 1913).

Sargent, C.S. *Manual of the Trees of North America* (Dover Press, New York, 1922, reprint 1961).

van Gelderen, C.J. and D.M. *Maples for Gardens* (Timber Press, Oregon, 1999).

van Gelderen, D. M., de Jong, P.C. and Oterdoom, H.J. *Maples of the World* (Timber Press, Oregon, 1995).

Veitch, J.H. *Hortus Veitchii* (London, 1906).

Vertrees, J.D. *Japanese Maples* (Timber Press, Oregon, 1987, 2nd Edition).

APPENDIX 3
USEFUL ADDRESSES

The Maple Society,
Secretary W.C. Noble,
164 Toms Lane,
Kings Langley, Hertfordshire,
England WD4 8NZ.

The Vine Weevil Advice Centre can be contacted at its website: www.vine.weevil.org.uk for help on dealing with these pests.

Biological pest controls are obtainable from:
Defenders Ltd, Occupation Road, Wye, Ashrod, Kent TN25 5EN.
Tel: (01233) 813121

APPENDIX 4
NATIONAL COLLECTIONS OF MAPLES

W.L. Banks, Hergest Croft Gardens,
Ridgebourne, Kington,
Herefordshire HR5 3EG.

Viscount Ridley, Blagdon,
Seaton Burn, Newcastle on Tyne,
Northumberland NE13 6DD.

APPENDIX 5
WHERE TO BUY MAPLES

Belgium

Pepinières C.E.C.E., Avenue Leopold III no.12, B-7130 Bray.

British Isles

The Plantfinder, which is published annually by the RHS in association with Dorling Kindersley, has lists of suppliers of most plants available in Britain, including maples.

Barthelemy & Co., The Nurseries, 262 Wimborne Road West, Staplehill, Wimborne, Dorset, BH21 2DZ.

Hippopottering Nursery, Doncaster, Yorkshire.

Mallet Court Nursery, Curry Mallet, Taunton, Somerset, TA3 6SY.

P.M.A Plants, West Hatch, Taunton, Somerset.

France

Pepinières Adelaine, Route d'Herry, 18140 La Chappelle Montlinard.

Italy

Fratelli Gilardelli Nursery, 20041 Agrate Brianza, Viale delle Industrie 21, Milan.

Netherlands

Dvd Maat Entcultures, Laag Boskoop 92, 2771 GZ Boskoop.

Firma C Esveld Rijneveld 72, 2771 XS Boskoop.

United States of America

Buchholz & Buchholz Nursery, 41840 SW Vandehey Road, Gaston, Oregon 97119.

Forest Farm, Ray and Peg Prag, 990 Tetherow Road, Williams, Oregon 97544-9599.

Wells-Medina Nursery, 8300 NE 24th Street, Medina, WA 98039.

Mountain Maples (Don and Nancy Fiers), PO Box 1329, Laytonville, California, 95454-1329.

Woodlanders, Inc., 1128 Colleton Avenue, Aiken, South Carolina 29801.

APPENDIX 6
WHERE TO SEE MAPLES

Belgium

Arboretum Kalmthout, Heuvel 2, 2920 Kalmthout.

Herkenrode Gardens, Bosveld 26, 3150 Wespelaar.

British Isles

Royal Botanical Gardens, Kew, Richmond, Surrey.

Sir Harold Hillier Gardens and Arboretum, Jermyns Lane, Ampfield, Near Romsey, Hampshire.

Savill and Valley Gardens, Windsor Great Park, Windsor, Surrey.

Thorpe Perrow Arboretum, Snape, Near Bedale, North Yorkshire.

Westonbirt Arboretum, Tetbury, Gloucestershire.

Winkworth Arboretum, Hascombe Road, Godalming, Surrey.

Former Czechoslovakia

Arboretum Mlynany of the Academy of Sciences of Slovakia.

Novy Dvur, near Opaca.

Pruhonice Park, 252 43 Pruhonice.

France

Arboretum des Barres, 45290 Nogent-sur-Vernisson, Loiret.

Arboretum de Chèvreloup, Rocquencourt, Yvelines.

Arboretum de Segrez, Saint Sulpice de Farière, Essonne

Jardins Botanique de Gondremer, 88700 Autrey, Vosges

Les Jardins de la Sedelle, Villejoint 23160, Crozant.

La Vasterival, Sainte Marguerite-sur-Mer, Seine-Maritime.

Germany

Botanischer Garden Rombergpark, 44225 Dortmund-Brünninghausen.

Tharandt, Forstbotanischer Garten der Universität, 01737 Dresden.

Bergpark Wilhelmshöhe, Kassel.

Staatspark Karlsaue, Kassel.

Ireland

Birr Castle, Birr, County Offaly.

John F. Kennedy Arboretum, New Ross, County Wexford.

Mount Congreve, Waterford, County Waterford.

National Botanic Gardens, Glasnevin, Dublin 9

Rowallane Garden, Saintfield, Ballynahinch, County Down.

Italy

Fratelli Gilardelli Nursery, 20041 Agrate Brianza, Viale delle Industrie 21, Milan.

Netherlands

Stichting Arboretum Trompenburg, Honingerdijk 86, 3062 NX Rotterdam.

Von Gimborne Arboretum, Vossesteinsesteeg, Doorn, 3508 TD Utrecht.

Poland

Institute of Dendrology, Kórnik, Near Poznan.

Slovenia

Radomlje, Ljubljana.

North America

Arnold Arboretum, 125 Arborway, Jamaica Plain, Massachusetts 02130.

Morris Arboretum of the University of Philadelphia, 9414 Meadowbrook Avenue, Philadelphia, Pennsylvania 19118.

Morton Arboretum, Lisle, Illinois.

New York Botanical Garden, 200th Street and Kazimiroff Boulevard, Bronx, New York 10458.

Strybing Arboretum and Botanical Gardens, Golden Gate Park, 9th Avenue and Lincoln Way, San Francisco, California 94122.

University of British Columbia, Vancouver, Canada.

US National Arboretum, 3501 New York Avenue, N.E. Washington DC 20002.

Washington Park Arboretum, University of Washington, 2300 Arboretum Drive East, Seattle, Washington 98195.

Willowwood Arboretum, 300 Longview Road, Chester Township, New Jersey 07930.

Former USSR

Batumi, Georgia.

St Petersburg Botanical Garden, St Petersburg, Russia.

Moscow Botanical Garden, Moscow, Russia.

INDEX

Page numbers in *italics* refer to illustration captions, those in **bold** refer to main entries.

ACKNOWLEDGEMENTS

Many kind friends have given their valuable time and help in preparation of this manuscript and completion of this book.

I am indebted to and thank Piers Trehane for his invaluable advice on nomenclature.

I am grateful to John Gallagher and Dick van der Maat for reading the manuscript and for their comments, I am also grateful to Peter Gregory for his help and for checking the nomenclature, particulary of the Japanese maples.

Mrs Derrick who typed the manuscript has been a tower of strength, putting up with my foibles.

Finally, a big thank you to my wife, Primrose, for all her encouragement and support.

The publishers wish to thank Lawrence Banks and Allen Coombes for their assistance.